Advanced P[
Mindful Conversatior.
Connect Deeply, Live Joyously

"In this concise, beautifully written book, Peter Gibb takes us beyond the traditional advice for how to talk to another person. He also teaches us how to connect with our selves, and more broadly, with our lives. He bravely opens up about his own successes and failures so that we might have more of the former. Throughout, Peter reveals the connections among mindfulness, self-acceptance and the meaning we make with others. If there are more important life skills, we don't know what they are."

Douglas Stone and Sheila Heen
Harvard Negotiation Project, authors of *Difficult Conversations:*
How to Discuss What Matters Most.

"Peter Gibb's wise, user-friendly manual on mindful conversation will help you talk to anyone, anywhere, about anything without anxiety or awkwardness. As a seasoned coach, consultant, and communications expert, Gibb brings decades of experience in mindfulness training to this witty, down-to-earth practicum for introverts and others who struggle with making themselves understood in social situations and feeling comfortable with their own voice. Effective, practical, and full of heart."

Mark Matousek
author of *Sex Death Enlightenment* and
When You're Falling, Dive: Lessons in the Art of Living

"I talk to people for a living – in interviews, workshops, and clients – and I have not read anything that looks this deeply and compassionately at conversation. Gibb not only understands the value of mindful, open-hearted communication, but offers clear, readable, and understandable tools for how to learn the everyday art of talking to anyone, whether a spouse, business associate, or stranger. Whether you're introvert, extrovert, or something in-between, you'll benefit from this wonderful book."

William Kenower
author of *Everyone Has What It Takes* and *Fearless Writing*

"Following his evocative memoir, *King of Doubt*, Peter Gibb has done it again with *Mindful Conversations*. Drawing on his hilarious sense of humor and gifts as a teacher and storyteller, Gibb manages to make what could be just another self-help book into an elegant invitation to... change your life. Seriously? Yes, indeed. For all the wit and self-deprecating stories, this is a serious book that calls on the reader to dig deep and find the courage to be not only a better conversationalist, but a transformed version of him or herself. This is a book with a heart that offers the reader a value-based primer on mindfulness and why it matters in calling forth our 'better angels.'"

Thomas J. Rice, Ph.D.
co-founder of The Interaction Institute for Social Change (IISC)
and author of *Far from the Land: An Irish Memoir*

"*Mindful Conversation* is a vital book for our times, weaving heartfelt encouragement, practical pathways, and accessible skills for creating meaningful interactions and relationships. It is the perfect, timely antidote for society's pandemic of isolation and loneliness."

Mary V. Gelinas, Ed.D.
author of *Talk Matters! Saving the World One Word at a Time* and
Managing Director of Gelinas James, Inc.

"Peter Gibb has pulled off a magic trick. He makes reading a book feel like an enlightening and joyful conversation with a compassionate and curious listener. In a world where digital exchanges of outrage isolate us, *Mindful Conversation* comes to the rescue with practical ideas for authentic expression and deep connection."

Jay G. Cone, Ph.D.
author of *The Surprising Power of Not Knowing What to Do* and
Founding Partner of Unstuck Minds

"Think of this book as a conversation that you want to have — and *need* to have. *Mindful Conversation* is about learning to speak openly and authentically, getting past awkward silences and unending small talk so that you can share your own story in a more compelling way. But it's also about listening deeply, asking questions, and truly understanding the people around you. Ultimately,

Peter Gibb's concise, smart, and engaging book is about connecting deeply and meaningfully — with others, with yourself, and with life."

Warren Berger, Author, A More Beautiful Question
and The Book of Beautiful Questions

"In *Mindful Conversation*, Peter Gibb offers a call to adventure for anyone seeking more conscious (and less stressful) communication. I'd like to rent a time machine to put this book in the hands of my tongue-tied younger self. But beyond its usefulness to the average person, this is a great resource for screenwriters and novelists who are trying to be mindful in the dialogue they put in their characters' mouths. With abundant examples of conversations both mindless and mindful, and clearly expressed principles and exercises, this book will have writers sharpening their dialogue to express the inner state of their characters and to show their development toward awareness. Whimsical drawings animate the concepts and the author's sharing of his own journey towards better communication skills makes this a useful and entertaining guide to mastering the art of conversation."

Christopher Vogler, Author,
The Writer's Journey: Mythic Structure for Writers

Other Books by Peter Gibb

King of Doubt, a memoir about overcoming
doubt and embracing the full life

Count on Spot, a Children's Board book

Mindful Conversation

Speak Openly, Connect Deeply, Live Joyously

PETER GIBB

atmosphere press

Published by Atmosphere Press

Cover design by Beste Miray

atmospherepress.com

To my students and coaching clients, dedicated,
brave and curious. Thank you for your faith in this work.
I celebrate your courage, your heart, and your progress
toward open expression, deep connection, and joy.
Your light shines ever bright in my sky.

Table of Contents

"Our oldest problem is the pain of separation, our deepest dream is the desire for reunion."

Susan Cain, author of *Quiet; Bittersweet*

"Look at every path closely and deliberately. Try it as many times as you think is necessary, then ask yourself, and yourself alone, one question ... Does this path have a heart? If it does, the path is good; if it doesn't, it is of no use."

Carlos Castaneda, *The Teachings of Don Juan*

Introduction

"Now that we've been introduced, let's have some fun."

Party goers joke and banter around a table covered by empty bottles and tossed napkins. A wobbly fellow – that would be me – clutches the table, a drowning man clinging to his raft.

Across the room, I spot a friend, laughing easily. I step in his direction, pull back. Heart thumping, sweat pooling, thoughts screeching: *You'll be the intruder, sound like a fool. Worse still, ignored.*

I lurch back to the table. A woman stands there, alone. I grab a plate, thrust it at her. "Cake?"

"Thanks, I have some." She displays her trophy.

"Yes. No. I mean." She's gone. The moment dies. And so do I.

That party was decades ago, but the feelings linger. Along with too many other similar moments.

I thought I was alone, an outsider, different. So wrong. My research shows that at least 25% of an average crowd feel uncomfortable in groups. 30% have a hard time speaking up.[1] Many struggle to create a conversation, stuck in unending, awkward, unsatisfying small talk. Not talking about what matters. Failing to engage in a meaningful way. Alone and anxious.

Conversation is the most central life skill that you never studied in school. Social conversation; business conversation; conversations with friends, strangers, brief exchanges, intimate dialogues – these are the oil that keeps life flowing. If the oil isn't there, the gears seize up. Thoughts don't flow. Stress builds. You feel isolated and disconnected. Anxiety and discontent gum up your engine.

Throughout history, the art of conversation has been fundamental to our existence and our evolution. Athenians who spearheaded the cradle of democracy in ancient Greece considered talk more vital than voting. Times change. In the U.S. now, we appear to be heading down a perilous road. Can our most basic, social assumption, Democracy, survive in a "post-conversational" society? Not just democracy. The family and the rule of law are equally threatened. Our way of life struggles to survive, and certainly not thrive, without constant, authentic, respectful conversation.

Struggles in everyday conversation can undermine our very identity – our relationship to ourselves, our self-confidence, motivation and ability to act with intention.

We yearn to connect and to express ourselves fully. It's baked into our DNA, paramount to our survival and position in the food chain. We know how to talk. We have the most advanced communication system in the animal kingdom: approximately 6,500 languages, 171,000 words in English alone[2], not to mention infinite variations when you add in gestures, tone, pitch, volume of voice, the whole range of non-verbal communication.

So, why such trouble? Why so much miscommunication?

o Lack of Awareness. You have to see what is possible before you can practice it.

o Lack of Role Models. Most of us model our communications on our family of origin. If you grew up with verbal abuse, non-listening, interruptions, repression of feelings, etc., then you are very likely to carry these patterns into your own adult communication style.

o Lack of Skill. If you've never been exposed to or learned how to speak and listen fully and openly, you can't imagine, much less practice this yourself.

o Resistance to Change. What's familiar is comfortable, even if it doesn't work.

Tools and Beyond

It's not just about the tools. Rather about our ability to use the tools. Your success with Mindful Conversation will grow from a blending of an inner shift (aka mindfulness) and an outer shift/new tools (aka conversation). Embracing Mindful Conversation requires gentle, persistent attention to both the inner and the outer.

I am an introvert. Early in my life, I thought that the solution was to become an extrovert. It took me decades to understand that I didn't need to be an extrovert. In fact, I had as much chance of becoming an extrovert as a snail has of becoming an eagle. Mindful Conversation is not about introversion or extroversion, but rather about how to fully and unabashedly embrace our deep need to express and connect.

Mindful Conversation is a path to wholeness and connection, but you must be willing to do the work: honor yourself and dare to speak about what matters to you. Open your heart and listen to others. It requires courage. And practice. The Czech novelist, Frank Kafka, called this human urge, the "hand outstretched in the darkness."

This book's mission is to encourage and assist you to connect and express yourself in a way that is unique and authentic for you. To talk about what matters to you, in a way that others will want to listen. To listen with the heart, you could say, and speak from the soul. The payoff is huge: at home, at work, with friends, with strangers, with family, with intimates, over the backyard fence or over the Internet.

Mindful Conversation is an invitation to a more full, free and joy filled life. Less stress, more fun, more productive.

More you.

More us.

More joy.

What do you long for?

If it's friends you're after, they're everywhere, but you have to meet and connect. Mindful Conversation will show you how to approach others respectfully and nonjudgmentally, and how to talk so they want to listen.

Or are you perhaps in an intimate relationship that is showing cracks? Enhance your conversation to reignite the spark, bring back the intimacy, and rejuvenate the connection that drew you together in the first place. Ideal, of course, is to work on your communications with your conversation partners (CP). But if that is not an option, changing your own rhythm can create new openings and delightful discoveries.

If you work in an organization, or you're in a leadership role at work or in your community, why not broadcast the invitation, "Let's Talk," as a way to build relationships and a spirit of collaboration? Use mindful conversation to foster teamwork and trust.

If you are a parent or part of a family, you are familiar with the challenges of family conversation. As David Brooks writes in his wonderful book *The Second Mountain,* "Never underestimate the power of the dinner table." Many kids these days grow up believing that text messaging is the path to closer friendship. The kind of connection I'm talking about can be augmented by technology, but it rarely happens solely via a screen. Still, the principles of Mindful Conversation apply both to face-to-face conversation and, with some adjustments, to your technology platform of choice.

You may already be practicing some of what is covered in this book. If so, *Mindful Conversation* will confirm and augment your desires for further growth. Or the ideas presented here may seem radical to you. You may have to stretch beyond your comfort zone. This requires an open mind. Mindful conversation can enhance any conversation, with anyone, about anything, anytime. It does not guarantee perfection. Mindful Conversation is about "human expression not human perfection." [3] It will substantially improve your odds for success. Experiment and then take what feels right and appropriate for you.

What is Conversation?

Dictionary definitions don't do it justice. We settle for so much less than what's possible.

We are social animals. We herd. We build vast cities, form tribes, raise families, grow organizations, create clubs, teams, political parties and dinner parties. We form relationships for survival, productivity, procreation and comfort. Conversation is the glue that helps us sustain these relationships. Conversation is more than talk; it is our identity on parade.

I define **conversation** as the master path to connection

7

and expression, the thread that links us to the moment, to ourselves, to one another, and to our shared humanity. Much more on this to come.

The word "conversation" usually conjures up a dialogue between yourself and one or more others. This is the Me - You (The First) conversation. The Me - You conversation links us to (or isolates us from) family and friends, colleagues and acquaintances. But there is so much more. Hidden inside each of us is the Me - Me (The Second) conversation, the conversation you have with yourself, that no one else knows about but yet deeply affects who you are and how you relate. Changes in the Me - Me conversation impact both the Me - You conversation and the Me – Us (The Third) conversation, our dance with the life force that holds us all together, our common humanity.

There are thus actually three distinct conversations, happening simultaneously, each impacting the other two. In this book, we will explore all three types of conversation, Me - - You (first), Me - Me (second), and Me - Us (third).

What is Mindfulness?

A few years ago, the term "Mindfulness" was relatively unknown in the western world. It conjured up images of a Buddha figure, eyes closed, legs crossed, beatific smile, thumbs to forefingers, sitting under the Boti tree. Mindfulness has now been embraced by millions in the west, thanks to overwhelming evidence of its effectiveness. But what is this thing called "Mindfulness"?[4] Here's my take:

"Mindfulness" refers to a state of being, characterized by present moment awareness, both of one's self (inner awareness, thoughts and feelings) and the world around (outer awareness, brought to us through the senses). Living mindfully means being grounded in the present moment, the 'now.' Mindfulness infers values such as compassion, non-judgmentalism, and a gentle acceptance of what is. Living mindfully

8

involves a sense of connection to the whole canvas of existence, a recognition that we are in this together. On the same team, all of us. We sink or swim together. Mindfulness is aspirational – always seeking an open heart and a calm mind.

Mindfulness is not multi-tasking; it is not trying to control or analyze everything; it is not following every whim, nor is it being held hostage by every fear that creeps into your being. Mindfulness is surrender. Not surrender as in to an enemy, but surrender into your authentic self, into the belly of the universe.

Mindfulness is not a synonym for meditation. Meditation is a practice that may help you become more mindful but not a requirement.

So, what is Mindful Conversation?

Mindful Conversation is a conscious approach to sharing our life experience, thoughts and feelings, dreams and desires, in words and gestures, with friends and strangers. Not everyone, of course, will play on this team. Some will continue to see life as a competition: "whatever you get is that much less for me." Mindful conversation is for you if you want a life filled by authentic expression, deep connection, and the joy of knowing that you are never alone because you are an overarching life force.

When you engage in conversation, you are a mini broad-casting station, sending your message out to the world. Every Mindful Conversation awakens the possibility of discovering a new friend, or rediscovering an old one, a lover, a business associate, a client, a teacher, a story, a passion, a purpose, a life. Mindful Conversation is a path to discovery, connection, and love, a path to becoming who you really are. It is a path of joy.

If you want a formal definition, here is as exact and precise as I can be:

Mindful Conversation is a means of verbal and non-verbal communication, part art, part science, and part way-of-being. It is designed to maximize potential for self- expression and connection, focused on exchanges about what matters most to the participants. Mindful Conversation includes methods to enhance change in both inner and outer realms. It encompasses connection on 3 distinct levels: Me - You, Me - Me, and Me - Us, as well as values and tools for listening, speaking and thinking.

When I reflect on this definition, I realize that I have defined a way of being. If so, then so be it. I believe that my drivers and joys are not that different from yours. We all want to express and connect about what matters to us. My wish is that Mindful Conversation may wrap you in as much life and hope as it has me.

Three Goals of Mindful Conversation

1. SPEAK OPENLY

Speaking Openly is about authenticity — coming out from behind the mask to show your real self. It doesn't mean wearing your heart on your sleeve or saying every thought or feeling that enters your mind. It does mean daring to be vulnerable, sharing your motivations and intentions, your "prouds" and your "sorries." It means talking with respect about yourself and inviting others to respond in kind.

2. CONNECT DEEPLY

Connecting deeply refers predominantly to listening in a new way. It means striving to understand others (and yourself), being patient enough to listen, not too proud to ask questions. It means abandoning Serial Monologue and Grabbing Responses, in favor of Reflective Listening. It means leading with empathy and respect, and attending with appropriate verbal and nonverbal tools of connection.

3. TALK ABOUT WHAT MATTERS

Mindful Conversation includes play and easy banter, but you can't avoid the big life issues, whatever they may be for you. If "small talk" is the only talk you make, then you can never be fully on the path of Mindful Conversation. Dare to talk about what matters. And, of course, you – and only you – can define what that is for you.

How is Mindful Conversation different?

How is Mindful Conversation (this book and this practice) different from other approaches to human communication.

o Most theories of conversation teach tools, but as psychologist Abraham Maslow said, "If the only tool you have is a hammer, then every problem looks like a nail." Your conversations soon become repetitive, forced and stilted. Mindful Conversation goes deeper. It includes an entire toolbox, but is based on values, the C.A.R.E. (Curiosity, Authenticity, Respect, Empathy) Model of human interaction.

○ Most theories of conversation consider only Me - You talk. Mindful Conversation includes the three levels of conversation already introduced:

- Me - You
- Me - Me
- Me – Us

This is a big stage to walk onto. The stage is set. The curtain is about to be opened. Are you ready?

○ Most theories of conversation talk about means and methods of conversation but give little attention to *what* you talk about. Mindful Conversation looks at how you speak, how you listen, and also, what you choose to talk about. It is about bringing the words, the music and the dance together, on the path to meaning.

Sources for this Book

This book draws from both my professional and personal experience, and my life-long passion for authentic connection. I grew up a shy, sensitive kid, then an awkward teen, and for too long, a bewildered adult. Most of the time, around others, I felt like an outsider, an introvert who longed to be an extrovert. I struggled for so many years, so many uncomfortable times. I watched and listened a lot, wondering how all those cool, relaxed others did it. I finally figured out some of the secrets, how little it had to do with introversion or extroversion. I recognized the distortions in my "story." I acknowledged that I was a good listener and that this was, in fact, a gift that I could give to those around me. Once I accepted my gift for listening, I discovered that I also had a lot to say. I told myself a new story, and in that moment, a new life was born. Mindful Conversation became my passion in life. I realized how many people suffered through the same struggles I had lived with for so long. I had to share my insights, the source now of such meaning, joy and confidence in life. This book is the result of that journey.

For 25 years, I consulted, lectured, taught workshops, wrote and coached individuals and organizations on the attitudes and skills discussed in this book. I have worked on 4 continents, in 16 countries and 3 languages, across cultures, in some of the world's largest corporations, as well with families, couples and individuals. I've worked in hospitals and banks, non-profits and government agencies, in third world countries, in the emerging democracies of Eastern Europe, and at the highest levels of government in the U.S.

The principles that I write about in this book are generally universal, but my choices are inevitably formed by my own biases, cultural conditioning, my gender, my life and work experiences, my ethnicity, and the privileged life I have led.

My "PhD" is in eavesdropping, in parks, airplanes, in meeting rooms, on the street and at the water cooler. I've also studied the psychology and the literature. Some of it is good, but too much misses the most fundamental truth, that every conversation is an opportunity for connection, expression, discovery and joy. Conversation is not just a problem to be solved.

Approach conversation from the viewpoint of possibility and you are a kid in a candy store.

I am still on a learning curve. I make plenty of mistakes. I get judgmental and impatient. Mindful Conversation is an aspiration I work towards, knowing I shall never fully master it. But I thrive on the path of lifetime learning.

Full disclosure: I am hardly neutral. Where I was once deathly afraid of conversation, I am now wildly, madly in love. This shift in attitude has transformed my life. Mindful

Conversation is my ticket to freedom, to being who I am meant to be, connected through love, a joyous traveler on this path of connection. Will you join me there?

How to "Read" This Book

This book is divided into five parts. I suggest you start with Part 1 to explore the territory. Then take it step by step, or jump around if you prefer. Patience and practice are essential. Be gentle and forgiving with yourself and your conversational partners (referred to as "CP's" throughout this book).

The five parts of your journey are:

Part 1. Explore the Territory

Part 2. The Me - You Conversation: Listen to Connect

Part 3. The Me - You Conversation: Speak to Express

Part 4. The Me - Me Conversation: Connect with Yourself

Part 5. The Me - Us Conversation: Connect with Life.

Each chapter begins with a "smile," an original cartoon, a bit of levity because you are the one doing the work and you deserve a smile. And, let's face it, conversation has lots of absurdities. I hope you smile often on your journey.

Each chapter ends with a standard format: **"Notes from the Journey"** and **"Next Steps."**

Notes from the Journey is a summary of the chapter, comprising:

1. Core Awareness: The essential mindset or attitude for success.
2. Core Value(s): The belief or reason behind why you may choose to follow the suggested steps.

3. Core Skill: The learnable behavior to practice

4. Core Tool: The specific steps that put the skill into action.

Next Steps consists of exercises, written and verbal, some social, some solitary. Many of these exercises can be easily integrated into your everyday life. If they feel awkward or you are reluctant to try something in public, you can do a lot privately. Or you might benefit by finding a traveling companion, or forming a Mindful Conversations group, for practice, camaraderie, and support.

I invite you also to keep a "Conversation Journal," a notebook for your reflections, as you experiment and become more conscious of your own conversation. Writing can help you see new points of view and solidify your learning.

Ready ... Set ...

Every conversation is an invitation to joy and an opportunity to rediscover the wonder, beauty and immense possibilities of life. Mindful Conversation is an emotional, intellectual, physical and spiritual journey.

Mindful Conversation is a way to dance with, rather than try to impress or manipulate others. Apply yourself to understanding and practicing Mindful Conversation, and you will find yourself more comfortable, relating in new ways, reclaiming the power of conversation and helping to rekindle the true spirit of a diverse, democratic society.

Mindful Conversation doesn't promise nirvana in every conversation. But if you adopt the spirit of Mindful Conversation, you will be on a lifetime learning path for connection, expression and growth. You will create and sustain more authentic and satisfying relationships – with others, with yourself, and with our common humanity.

Writing this book has been a personal labor of love for me.

I welcome your feedback, thoughts and experiences with Mindful Conversation. I offer various workshops, talks, blogs and coaching. Please visit my web site, www.petergibb.org or contact me, peter@petergibb.org if you wish to connect further.

This book can point you in the right direction and urge you forward, but it can't do the work for you. That's your job.

And you can do it.

GO!

Part 1

Explore the Territory

Chapter 1
Shift From Talk to Conversation

"I had a great conversation with my daughter yesterday. I forget what we talked about. I was brilliant. She nodded a lot."

Q. "Where is the nearest gas station?"

A. "Straight ahead, two blocks."

This conversation is a straightforward exchange of fact.

The subject is clear. The dynamics are simple. Such conversations are a helpful part of everyday life. We ask. We (usually) receive.

But conversation often involves far more than facts. There are verbal and non-verbal signals, sometimes with similar messages, sometimes in contradiction to each other. There are emotions, hopes and fears. There are relationships, past, present, future. Power dynamics. Who's calling the shots? What's at stake? There is the environment, suitable or not? And in our era, always lurking somewhere, technology, the use or abuse thereof. This complex tapestry of issues, while often not overtly mentioned, is frequently the sub-text, what participants are really thinking about. Spoken words can quickly become a mask we hide behind.

> Ashley: Did you take the dog out?
>
> Harry: I took her out this morning. It's your turn.
>
> Ashley: So, you keep track? Do you take notes too?
>
> Harry: This is an equal opportunity house.
>
> Ashley: Very funny.

What is this conversation about? If you answered, "Taking the dog out," try again.

Mindful Conversations

Mindful Conversations are multi-dimensional, engaging the whole person: mind, heart, body and spirit. Conversation is enormously complex. A lot can go wrong because a lot is often at stake. But when conducted skillfully, Mindful Conversation is the crucible for connection and expression – deeper understanding, more satisfying and trusting relationships, better decisions, creativity, discovery, growth, and joy. Such conversations, when skillfully managed and conducted with heart, will increase your chances for success in every aspect of your life. The joy will follow in more ways than I can enumerate.

Too often what the speakers are really thinking about is never even put on the table. *Am I O.K.? Does she like me? How can I bring up the subject of the money? Why does he talk to me in that tone of voice?* A Mindful Conversation can be nominally about any subject. When the real subject is unearthed in respectful and empathic language, the conversation transforms from formulaic fake talk into a dance of connection and discovery.

Let's examine a typical, connecting conversation to see what happens.

MEET STEVE AND MARTHA

Martha and Steve are neighbors, casual acquaintances. They meet at a neighborhood social.

Steve: "Hi, Martha. Haven't seen you in a while."

Martha: "I don't get out the way I used to. Charlie just started kindergarten. He's a great kid, a bundle of energy, cute, smart, like I say, a great kid, but oh my, I'm so –"

Steve: "Kindergarten. Wow. Next thing you know, he'll be a teenager. I have two teenage girls in the house. Enjoy the little ones while you can."

Martha: "I have to work too. I get up at 5:30 to get everything ready, then leave the house at 7:20."

Steve: "5:30, phew, I couldn't do that. Never been an early morning guy myself."

Martha: "Working and being a single mom, it's not so easy you know. Getting up at 5:30, and often I can't get to bed before 11. I want the best for Charlie, but I have to work. I hate to leave him. I'm at my wits end. I don't know if I can –"

21

Steve: "I know how hard it is. Harriet and I hired a nanny. The best; I can give you the agency number. It'll change your life. Speaking of Harriet, that must be her calling my cell now. I promised I'd pick her up. Sorry, gotta go."

This conversation starts on a normal, friendly tone. If you were analyzing the exchange, how would you characterize it? What is this conversation really about? How would you describe the dynamics?

Serial Monologue

Martha and Steve are miles from Mindful Conversation. They are engaging in what I call Serial Monologue. Serial Monologue is not really conversation at all, and certainly not connection.

Both Martha and Steve are focused inward. The conversation is "me" focused. There is no "we." What the other is saying is mostly irrelevant. A graphic representation looks like this:

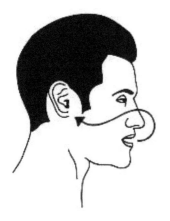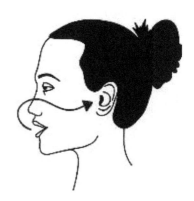

In Mindful Conversation, each is engaged with what the other is saying. The conversation is "we" focused. Graphically, more like this:

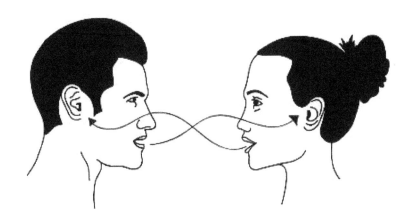

Martha and Steve, talking in Serial Monologue,[5] are both distracted; they interrupt; they undercut and disregard one another; they compete for time, topic and attention. Whereas two people in Mindful Conversation are like dancers, Steve and Martha are more like competing football players, both sides trying to grab the ball and score points on some mythical scoreboard. They talk *at* one another rather than *with* one another. They don't want to, don't know how to, or don't have the patience to listen. There is no real connection, no support, little learned and no understanding.

Do you know anyone who talks like this?

We were given two ears but just one mouth. Might this be a message?

Most people who talk consistently in Serial Monologue are unaware of their own pattern of conversation. Could this be why so many of us stumble along under the curse of isolation and polarization? No listening equals no connection equals no understanding.

Serial Monologue may distract us briefly from our worries,

but ultimately it is a lonely path. Hoping to be understood when no one is listening is like tossing a stone into an empty pond, then waiting for the ripples.

In Serial Monologue, we are attending to our own inner chatter, or planning our response, or thinking about what to prepare for dinner tonight. Based on my research, Serial Monologue substitutes for conversation in about 50% of conversation.

> Wise men speak because they have something to say; fools because they have to say something.
> **Plato**

Grabbing Response

Serial Monologues feature the **Grabbing Response**. One person grabs the topic from the other and typically redefines it, to their desire. The new speaker takes over (or tries to) telling his story, giving her opinion, or dictating the topic. Back and forth goes the focus, dropped, fumbled, confused, like the football in a game played by small children.

At the beginning of Martha and Steve's conversation, Martha is struggling, probably feeling overwhelmed. Steve offers two words of lukewarm interest in her remarks. Then he grabs the subject (Charlie, and Martha's role as mother) and converts it into something new (how difficult it is to raise teenage girls, and how he is a more experienced parent than Martha). Martha is out. Steve is in.

Although the grabber is often unaware of what he is doing, the deeper message is any or all of the following:

1.   I am not interested in what you have to say.

2. I have something more interesting / relevant / amusing to discuss.
3. I want to be the center of attention. You should listen to my story / advice / opinion.
4. I know more about this than you do. I can fix your problem better than you can.
5. It's a waste of my time to listen to you.

Many people speak entirely through grabbing responses. In effect, such speakers put themselves at the center of every exchange. Understanding and connection are not even remotely possible.

The kind of unsolicited advice that Steve offers, is a waste of time or worse. Steve is speaking from his own, unconscious bias, giving advice without bothering to understand Martha's concerns. Martha will most likely see his unsolicited advice is as condescending, unhelpful and irritating disruption.

Grabbing responses are lightly disguised forms of domination. Serial Monologues are a battleground where adversaries pout and shout, "Me. Me. Listen to me. I know what's best. I have the power. I am the one." Mindful Conversation, by contrast, creates a meeting ground where creativity and support flourish, a field where ideas and positive connections grow, a stage where there are no losers because it is not a competition. Not me versus you, but you and me listening and supporting each other.

Reflective Listening

An alternative to Serial Monologue and the grabbing response is **Reflective Listening**. Reflecting is to Mindful Conversation as breathing is to life, essential and never ending. Responding reflectively radically shifts the sense of ownership, the depth, and the tone of conversation.

A **Reflective Response** demonstrates interest and/or understanding in the topic and the speaker. It reinforces, or further explores the speaker's message. A Reflective Response deepens the conversation and strengthens the connection between the Conversational Partners (CP's).

Successful reflective listening requires focus, intention, and skill. You need to:

1. Have the intention and presence of mind to take in the full measure of your CP, not to reply automatically with your own story or advice.

2. Attend to both the spoken (words, tone, pitch) and the unspoken (eye contact, facial expression, body language, posture) message.

3. Respond to your CP in one or more of three ways:

    A. Attending quietly, using gestures such as head nodding, simple murmurs of acceptance like "OK" or "I see"; or demonstrating that you have received the message through facial expression or body language.

    B. Repeating back your CP's actual words, or your understanding of what you heard, or inferred.

    C. Inquiring to help clarify or explore what was said.

You cannot do any of this without listening, really listening. Reflective listening is not stony silence. Nor does it mean that you agree with or approve of all that you hear, but it does signal that you heard and tried to understand what was said, and that you are interested in the speaker's spoken, and even the unspoken, message. Reflective responding has little in common with the most typical conversational modes, such as judging, advice giving, storytelling, shifting the topic, mocking, interrupting, distractedly multi-tasking, or wandering off into other universes.

Responding reflectively is more than a skill. It is a way of being, a habit, and a bedrock tool of Mindful Conversation.

Reflective responding is not sitting numb and waiting for your turn to speak. It always includes reflection and thought. It usually includes words and often non-verbal responses, such as body posture, facial expression, and appropriate touch.

Reflective listening is clearly NOT the only way to respond. There is, of course, also speaking. We'll get to that. But first, the great, so frequently neglected, land of listening.

REFLECTIVE VS ACTIVE LISTENING

You may know the term "active listening." Reflective listening builds on active listening but goes beyond it. (A comparison is contained in Chapter 8.) The specifics of how to develop into a dynamic reflective listener are covered in detail in Part 2 of this book. There, you will learn when and how to use reflective responses skillfully and empathically to open a treasure chest of personal rewards. You will form deeper, faster, more satisfying and balanced relationships with family, friends, customers and colleagues.

Others are likely to pick up on that and respond in kind. You will become more sought out, someone whom others delight in talking with and sharing what's important to them. Your status, power and influence in the world should also rise as others will *want to be* on your team. You will be more creative and open, engaging with other people and new ideas in fresh ways.

Inspiration and new energy may gravitate to you from

seemingly unlikely sources. Rather than being something that you fear or shy away from, conversation will become one of life's great pleasures.

STEVE'S OPTIONS: POSSIBLE REFLECTIVE RESPONSE

Let's see how different Steve and Martha's conversation could have been, had Steve used reflective, instead of grabbing responses. Remember that after Martha's opening remark about her son Charlie, Steve said, "Kindergarten. Wow. Next thing you know, he'll be a teenager. I have two teenage girls in the house. Girls are so much harder to raise than boys."

This classic grabbing response could have been replaced with any one of many **reflective comments**, such as:

o "You've got your hands full. Sounds overwhelming."

o "How's Charlie doing in kindergarten? How's his mom doing?"

o "It's been a while since I've had a kindergartner. What's it like these days?"

o "You really love Charlie, don't you? You're trying your best to do right by him."

These are just a few of hundreds of possible reflective responses. Take a moment now and write five other reflective responses that Steve could have made. (He needs the help.) How do you think you would have responded if you were Steve? (Note: If you haven't already, now could be a great time to inaugurate your conversational journal.)

Effective and frequent reflecting, more than any other single action, will create understanding and connection between you and your conversational partners (CP's). It is basic, essential, and never ending. If you have little or no experience with reflective responding, you'll need to practice until it becomes as automatic as breathing.

LIMITS OF REFLECTIVE RESPONSE

I do not mean that you should always respond reflectively. Parity of speaking and listening is a major principle of Mindful Conversation. You get to talk too. (Discussed in detail in Part 3.) But if talking is all you do (minimal listening), then you are majoring in Serial Monologue, not Mindful Conversation.

What if ...

It's not always clear or simple or even possible to engage in lengthy reflective listening.

If Steve is interested, but doesn't have time right now, far better to say so than to pretend. "I know this is an important issue for you, Martha, (a brief reflective response) but I have to pick up Harriet. Could we set up another time to talk?"

Note that in this example, he shows respect for Martha and reinforces his genuine interest in her situation. But what if Steve is <u>not</u> interested in Martha's parenting problems? Can he be both respectful and authentic now?

Steve could say: "I can tell this is an important issue for you, Martha. I'm no expert on parenting either. Perhaps we can think of someone who could be a better person for you to talk with."

Each of these responses shows authenticity, respect and empathy, 3 of the core values in the C.A.R.E. model. Steve is direct and authentic. He is not agreeing with her approach nor judging her, and nor is he advising her, or telling his own story. Even though he cannot help with this particular problem, the relationship, Martha's self-respect and their friendship live to see another day.

Reflective Responding requires bringing your full self to the listening. You can't fake curiosity or empathy. More on all of this in Part 2 of this book.

Notes from the Journey

Core Awareness: Mindful Conversation is distinguished from Serial Monologue by the frequent use of reflective listening.

Core Values: Respect. Paying close attention to what another says is a constant gift of respect.

Core Skill: Resisting the impulse to default to your own story, joke, judgment or advice.

Core Tool: Reflective Listening, mirroring back to someone what you have heard or infer from what they have said.

Next Steps

1. Notice when and how frequently so many people rely on Serial Monologue and grabbing responses as their basic model of conversation. Be aware of grabbing responses in your own conversation. In your conversation journal, write your own observation notes and comments on the frequent use of Serial Monologue and grabbing responses. Why do you think people speak this way? What impact do you think it has on relationships? Do you speak with Grabbing Responses "Never, seldom, sometimes or often"?

2. Seek a partner who might be interested in practicing these skills with you. (You can tell them what you're doing, or keep your learning private.) If you feel particularly brave, ask this partner (or anyone who knows you well enough) to give you some feedback about your listening. Be curious! When they give you feedback, use this as an opportunity to practice reflective listening. Repeat back, summarize what they are saying. Ask questions to understand more. Have a conversation about conversation.

Chapter 2
Focus on the Core

"I don't know what it is, but it seems to be part art, part science, and part being."

A Breakthrough Experience

It was the first cold day of winter. My business partners and I sat in a small conference room in San Francisco. We had squirreled ourselves away, shaping plans that would determine whether our company would thrive or dive. So much on the line – the company, my career, my financial investment. But for me, something even more important at stake, swirling just beneath my awareness.

I struggled to follow the discussion. A dark cloud descended.

I tracked how frequently each of my partners spoke. My inner critic shifted into overdrive. The only voice I could hear was my brain imploding. *Why am I so uncertain? So useless.* I disappeared into a dark pit of anxiety. *I am not suited for this work.* My mind mocked me, like an old crow on a high branch, dripping with judgment.

When the others took a break, I sat numb in my chair. I turned to one of my partners, whom I trusted deeply. I gulped and blurted out how overwhelmed I felt, how I'd lost my tongue, couldn't follow the discussion. "Am I too quiet? How will I be perceived?" I asked, desperate for recognition that I was okay.

David paused. My identity hung on his response. "Well, you run the risk of being seen as irrelevant."

I slunk deeper into my chair. I looked into his eyes to see if there was more. The others were returning. I escaped into the restroom. As a long time meditator, I knew the power of breathing and letting go. The habit returned to me. I slowed down. *Breathe in, breathe out.* With each out breath, I whispered to myself, *Let Go, Let Go.* A piece of the anxiety fell away, like cold mud in a warm shower. For the first time, I could hear myself think. The only authentic path: admit my overwhelm; confess my confusion; ask appropriate questions.

Back in the room, I tentatively presented my confusion. To my delight, another partner echoed my feeling. We engaged in the question. My fears began to fall away. I spoke with more clarity. For the first time, I could let go of my anxiety and speak openly. A spirited, thoughtful discussion followed, concluding in a consensus of insight and direction.

At the end of the meeting, we debriefed our process (as we always did). David turned to me, "Peter, you made us see what we were missing, the assumption that locked us into the past. Your question turned it around. Thank you. Deeply." Others echoed in a kind of chorus. I breathed again. In, out. Ah.

I smiled and gave thanks that I had partners who gave me straight talk and that I had spoken my simple truth. All I did was to speak authentically and raise a question that I was curious about. All I did was all that was required: to speak openly, and thereby move the conversation forward.

I went home, feeling whole again. The company survived and went on to flourish.

I learned a lot that day, about curiosity, and authenticity and the value of vulnerability, big lessons for one day. The concept of "Mindful Conversation" began to form in my mind.

Psychological Safety

In subsequent years I learned much more about the concept of "psychological safety" in work environments. Through my own consulting work and from books like Amy Edmondson's *The Fearless Organization*, I have come to appreciate how essential workplace psychological safety is to success in today's ever changing business world. I have watched the challenges in creating work cultures where people are invited and encouraged to speak out and listen in. I have witnessed the costs of not achieving psychological safety. And I have seen how modeling and spreading the concept of mindful conversation in an organization is the single best way to enhance psychological safety at work.

The Core

Mindful Conversation is a journey of discovery: part art, part science, part being. Where these overlap, meaning and magic await.

The **Science** of Mindful Conversation is a set of behaviors that

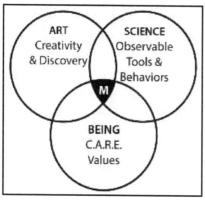

can be described, taught, observed and practiced. These behaviors don't guarantee Nirvana, but they enormously improve the odds for better relationships, more productive conversation, satisfaction and joy.

The **Art** of Mindful Conversation is in the mix, where the science meets the spirit of the speakers, in a dance of creativity and discovery. Every conversation, like every piece of art, is different. The artist weaves them together to create meaning. **Being** refers to the principles of mindfulness, brought into conversation. The heart of this mindful practice lies in the four primary values of Mindful Conversation, the C.A.R.E. Model: Curiosity, Authenticity, Respect and Empathy.

When Art, Science and Being come together, **Meaning and Magic** appear. The right people start showing up in your life.

Relationships that were troubled begin to heal. Creativity flows. You open to being inspired, and so you are inspired. Answers to vexing problems appear. There's a sense of peace within that opens the floodgate of hope and possibility. Come for the results, stay for the magic.

The Values

At its most basic, mindful conversation consists of listening and speaking. We use these two "meta-processes" to connect to ourselves, to others, and to the life and species into which we are born. At the core of Mindful Conversation is a set of four values, the C.A.R.E. model.

1. **C** - Curiosity
2. **A** - Authenticity
3. **R** - Respect
4. **E** - Empathy

Curiosity is the doorway to learning, growth, and new experience. Approaching a person (yourself or another) with curiosity communicates that you want to know their story, to understand who they are and what's important to them.

Approaching an experience with curiosity throws open the door, wide onto life itself. Curiosity is your ally on the path of discovery.

Authenticity grounds us in our own being, in the present moment. It dramatically reduces the stress of living in the past or the future. Authenticity opens you up to your external, sensory experiences (sights, sounds, smells, tastes, and touch) and to your internal experience (thoughts and feelings). Authenticity frees you to engage unapologetically and fully. Discard the mask. Let your true colors shine.

Respect levels the playing field. It acknowledges the inherent worth in all life. Respect is evident when kindness and compassion consistently win out over judgment and fear. We earn respect by giving it to others. We can disagree, even disapprove or feel angry with another, and yet treat them with respect.

Empathy is the ability to understand and relate to another person's feelings and perspective. It is the window into another's soul, the doorway to deep connection. Empathy is the glue that holds it all together.

These values are not a multiple choice test. Mindful Conversation is the blending of all four.

These four values appear along a spectrum, not in any on / off duality. But let's examine the feeling / tone generated when these values are absent (unconscious conversation, Column A below) versus the feeling / tone generated by the presence of each of these four values (mindful conversation, Column B below).

	A **Unconscious** **Conversation** **(Absence of this value)**	**B** **Mindful** **Conversation** **(Presence of this value)**
Curiosity	I feel isolated from new experience. Closed minded.	I seek and am enriched by new experience. Open minded.
Authenticity	I am protective, defensive and fearful. Often rooted in past or future.	I am revealing and emboldened. Rooted in my unique being, here and now.
Respect	I ignore, attack or demean others, creating insecurity and isolation.	I help others feel safe, acknowledged and whole.
Empathy	I relate to others as "them." I feel separate and alone.	I recognize others as like myself, part of the universal web of humanity. I am connected to a larger whole.

Throughout this book, we will be learning and practicing tools, behaviors, language and gestures. But if the tools are "performed" absent the values, they quickly become hollow and counterproductive. This is what frequently happens with Active Listening. Mindful Conversation is not about winning or proving that you are smarter, stronger, richer, more worldly or more spiritual. Mindful Conversation shifts the conversational norm from competition to connection. It reduces stress in high anxiety exchanges such as first dates, job interviews, high stakes meetings and conflicts, and anytime you feel like an outsider.

Digging for Treasure

Let's revisit our friends Steve and Martha again. Think of their conversation as digging for hidden treasure. They start at the surface. Surface work is usually focused on **external facts.** This is where many conversations start and stop. This is the face that we too often show to the world. The important facts (from Martha's point of view) are clear. She is a single, working mom with 2 children, one of whom just started kindergarten. Charlie seems a bit out of control. We can assume that Steve has heard and understood these facts, which are, nominally, the focus of the conversation.

Mindful Conversation takes us deeper, digging down through the hard dirt, the rocks and roots, into a deeper level of exploration, beyond just the facts, into the world of thoughts, still deeper into feelings, and finally into the world of personal meaning. The message here may be spoken, but is often hidden underneath the spoken words. The deeper layers may uncover deeper fears and insecurities. Although Martha cares deeply about Charlie and her role as mom, the only time she mentions how she feels is near the end, "I'm about at my wits' end." Steve never acknowledges this comment. Martha's feelings remain buried.

If we keep digging, we may uncover an even deeper truth, the **Personal Meaning**[6] or the significance that Martha attributes to the subject being discussed. We are now talking about unconscious beliefs and biases, personal images of how we see ourselves, the stories we tell ourselves about who we are or want to be.

Many people are not even aware that they are telling themselves a story. But we all do. Martha's story may include her confidence (or lack of) as a single mom. It may encompass dreams for a different kind of life, or concerns she has for Charlie. Martha's personal meaning might be about something going on at work that is interfering with her home life. It could even be about deep insecurities left over from childhood, "stories" that she is stupid or not lovable, too fat, too thin, or just too weird.

Lurking beneath our public persona, these three tiers wait to be tapped.

THE PYRAMID OF CONNECTION [7]

Like an iceberg. At the top, the visible facts are vital, but they are only the tip. Beneath the surface lie the deeper truths: thoughts, feelings and personal meaning, where

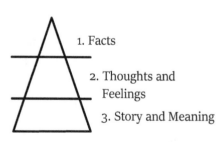

1. Facts

2. Thoughts and Feelings

3. Story and Meaning

deep satisfaction and disappointment dwell, where art, science and mystery overlap to create connection and magic. Mindful conversationalists listen for clues, and respond appropriately, reflecting, inquiring, attending, waiting, with curiosity and empathy, authenticity and respect. This is not to say that every conversation needs to or even should get to such a level. It is to say that if you want the full richness of connection and expression, you need to know how to speak this language and pick up the signals when others are ready to share themselves with you. If you lack these skills, or are hidden behind protective walls of fear and isolation, then you are unable to "talk about what matters."

Mindful conversations build great relationships. When you listen with the ears of your heart, you invite your CP's into the Magic of Connection.

Notes from the Journey

Core Awareness: The C.A.R.E model consists of four values (Curiosity, Authenticity, Respect, Empathy) that form the foundation for Mindful Conversation.

Core Value: Authenticity calls us to remove the mask and talk more about what really matters to us in life.

Core Skill: Understanding the balancing act, weaving an appropriate tapestry of art, science and being.

Core Tool: The Pyramid of Connection. At the top, are the facts, often discussed and visible. Deeper, lie thoughts and feelings, often not even mentioned. At the deepest level is the Personal Meaning, the story you tell yourself about yourself.

Next Steps

1. Think about / talk about / write about (plus whatever other forms of expression you wish) the C.A.R.E. model. What does it mean for you? Which value is easiest for you? Where are you challenged? What aspects of the model most align with your personal values? Are there parts that you are conflicted about?

2. Choose one of these four values that you would like to emphasize more in your conversation. Think, write, talk, draw (or use any form of expression) about the value. Define an opportunity for incorporating this value more robustly into your conversation. Develop a specific action plan. How will you hold yourself accountable? How will you reward yourself when you follow through?

Chapter 3
Understand Your Style

"For a while, my Observer felt left out after noticing your Explorer wink at my Performer, but then my Nurturer swooped in to save the day, and meanwhile, the soup got cold."

We each have a style of walking. And a style of talking.

You might have a hard time defining their conversation style. It's too familiar to notice, part of who you are, like breathing. Your "conversation style" is a collection of attitudes, habits, skills, feelings and preferences for relating to others in a way that is most natural and comfortable for you.

44

Your style is one primary influence on how you converse. A second significant influence is the unique circumstance of a particular interaction – whom you are talking with, the roles and relationships involved, the topic, your mood, the setting, time available, etc.

In any given conversation, the unique circumstances of that particular conversation plus your default conversation style merge to determine how you will actually show up. To become more mindful in your conversation, a useful first step is to become more aware of your natural style. You can then choose to further develop and rely on that style, or you can explore ways to migrate to, or include aspects of, other styles.

Conversational roles change rapidly and frequently; moods fluctuate, topics come and go; but at any one time, you are either listening and reflecting, speaking ... or sleeping.

We all want something from each conversation we're involved in. It may be to play center stage, or it may be to hide as inconspicuously as possible; it may be to learn, to connect, or to have fun; it may be to understand; or it may be to put someone down, to win the fight. Merging our desires with our roles (listening or speaking), we can identify four basic styles.

Before reading any further, I encourage you to try the Conversational Style Guide (CSG). This should take you 10 - 15 minutes. The guide and the personal report that follows are awareness building tools, to help you understand your current style of conversation, your satisfaction with your current style, and how to venture into alternate styles when and if you desire. If you like temperament and style type assessments, such as Myers Briggs or the Enneagram, you will enjoy this also. Some find such tools frustrating or overly restrictive. If this is you, you may also find this one frustrating. Use it or not, your choice. Get started at this link:

https://survey.alchemer.com/s3/5989413/4d7074977c7e

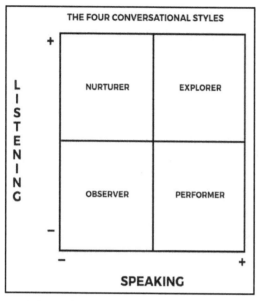

THE FOUR CONVERSATIONAL STYLES

Once you have completed and submitted your responses, you will receive a customized report back by email, explaining your relationship to each of the four styles and some initial suggestions for change, should you wish to experiment with new behaviors.

There is NO RIGHT OR WRONG STYLE. Each style has its strengths and limitations. The four styles do not represent baked-in types that you were born and are forever stuck with. Rather they are comprised of learned attitudes, habits, behaviors and skills that serve you or don't.

The four conversational styles are as follows:

1. The "observer" prefers to watch and reflect, and tends to be reserved in conversation, with an inward focus.

2. The "performer" prefers to speak out and be heard with a focus on him/herself.

3. The "nurturer" prefers to listen and support others, with an outward focus.

4. The "explorer" enjoys both speaking and listening and varies focus on self and others.

At various times, in various different settings, most of us

have dabbled in each of these styles. All four styles can add a critical dimension to any conversation. For example, at any one moment, you might be telling a story, in your performer role, but if you notice someone struggling or seemingly left out, you might slip into a nurturer role to try to draw them in. You can, with practice and motivation, move in the direction of any of the four styles.

As we move from left to right in the matrix, we move from more listening and reflecting oriented to more speaking. Thus, the performer typically speaks more than the observer, while the nurturer is usually more quiet than the explorer. And as we move from bottom to top, we move from being more self-focused to being more other focused. Thus, the observer may focus more on herself, wondering if she is fitting in or being left out, while the nurturer is more other focused, noticing that someone else has been left out of the conversation. The explorer is more we focused, and the performer, more me focused.

Each of the four styles can be played to an extreme, or can be moderate. For example, I have an acquaintance who shows up as an extreme performer. I'll call him Sam. Sam thrives on being the center of attention, has a stock of jokes and stories ready for any situation, and will keep entertaining until his audience disappears. My default mode of conversation with Sam is to fall into observer mode, listening to a few stories, and then (feeling resentful at the one-sided conversation), excuse myself. Over time, I have learned that relying too heavily on my observer role (which in this case makes me feel like an outsider and less like a participant) feeds his need, but does nothing for mine. I have also learned that I need to strongly assert my explorer side when I am with Sam, first by listening but then by signaling to him that I do not intend to roll over and routinely applaud while he dominates the conversation the entire time. In other words, I want to be in the conversation with respect for Sam, but also authentic in expressing my own desires to talk, not only to be the listener.

Each of the four styles has a focus and a driving question:

Nurturer	Explorer
Focus: You	Focus: Us
Question: Do I understand you? How can I support you?	Question: Are we achieving our purpose? How can I help us be successful?
Observer	**Performer**
Focus: Me, how I feel.	Focus: Me, how others perceive me.
Question: Am I included? Do I belong?	Question: Are others noticing me? How can I express myself?

Let's take a look at each of the four styles. Circumstances (e.g., Is the conversation with a close friend or a stranger? Is it a work setting or a social one? Is this a routine conversation or a particularly stressful one? Am I motivated to explore the dynamics? Is there time?) obviously influence how you behave. But as you read through the styles, think about your default style. Where are you most comfortable? Where do you go when you're feeling uncertain or lost? Which style do you fall naturally into, and which do you have to work to achieve?

The Observer

Whether listening or speaking, the observer's default communication style is restrained and quiet. The observer watches, taking it all in, scanning, reflecting, sifting. Think of the observer as a journalist, gathering facts and theories but not yet ready to release the story. When she is ready, she has a lot to say. In the meantime, she is watching and analyzing. Most observers prefer small, intimate settings to larger groups.

The question that the Observer often asks herself is, "Am I included. Do I belong?" The Observer is acutely aware of herself and whether she is genuinely included (or not) in the group or conversation. This inner dynamic can affect her comfort level, enjoyment of, and satisfaction with any conversation or meeting.

An observer's value to the larger conversation or group stems often from her being able to step back, notice what is going on, and identify important aspects of a given topic or dynamic. The observer is more contemplative and reflective than expressive. She may be the first to perceive what others are feeling or thinking but not saying. The observer often adds a calming influence that is beneficial, particularly in difficult conversations, where others are overly emotional and unable to see beyond their own points of view.

A limitation of being strongly identified as an observer is that others may wonder if you are engaged at all. If you wait too long to speak, the time may pass without your voice being heard. Your calm exterior presence can be healing for others, but your reticence may be mistaken for indifference.

If you are in your observer role and wish to challenge yourself and step out a bit into one of the other roles but are feeling unsure, take a moment to visualize yourself in a different role, for example as a nurturer. Think of the question that your nurturer self might ask, then try it. For example, "I want to be sure I understand what you've said. I heard some hesitation in your voice when you talked about your relationship with X. Can you elaborate?"

The Nurturer

Like the observer, the nurturer is generally more comfortable listening than speaking. The prime difference is that the nurturer focuses his energy externally, onto other people, ideas or events. The nurturer's primary tools are attending, paying attention to what is spoken and what is not, then using reflective listening and open-ended questions to draw others out.

The Nurturer finds satisfaction and meaning in his ability to encourage and care for others. As a result, he feels a sense of connection and inclusion. The questions that the Nurturer asks himself are, "What is X trying to say? What is underneath the words? Do I understand you? How can I support you?" The Nurturer encourages all voices to be heard and, as such, helps build a sense of unity. The Nurturer recognizes that many people feel intimidated or like an outsider from time to time. You can recognize the Nurturer from the quality of listening — genuine, deep and helpful.

The Nurturer's strengths are pretty obvious (how can you not appreciate one who listens and is then supportive?), but his limitations are important to pay attention to also. While nurturing is a very helpful activity, it can also become a mask to hide behind. If I nurture exclusively, I don't need to show much of myself or be vulnerable. I can keep the attention off of me. A Nurturer who only listens and supports others to the exclusion of sharing himself and his own vulnerabilities may lose touch with his own voice, to a point that he is not even aware of his own feelings or needs.

One natural path for the Nurturer to expand his comfort zone can be to experiment deliberately with his opposite, the Performer. Practice the art of storytelling (See Chapter 15 for details), and make a commitment to yourself to develop a story or two and tell them within the week. This may feel like an intimidating assignment. Find some aspect of storytelling that you enjoy or a way to reward yourself once you've tried.

The Performer

The Performer's great strength is that she has stories and opinions and is not afraid to share them. She can be entertaining, stoking the conversation with input and passion. Many performers are good at sharing their feelings, revealing more of the internal story, so it may be easier to get to know them. What you see is what you get. Performers put it out there: what they need, what they think, how they feel.

Performers often seem to exude confidence and lack self-consciousness, but this can be a screen. Stories and jokes and excessive talk can also cover over as much as they reveal.

The Performer often asks herself the question, "Am I the focus of attention. How can I be the star of this show?" She puts a lot of energy into the group, because she knows that a star must shine brightly.

The Performer is the opposite profile from the Nurturer. A full-on performer has no trouble being the center of attention, and is happy to talk about herself for extended periods of time without feeling self-conscious. Performers and Nurturers can feed on each other, the Performer getting more and more into her stories and opinions while the Nurturer is an attentive audience.

The conversational limitation of many performers is that they are so into their performance, they have little awareness of their impact on others. Some Performers become extreme serial monologuers. No matter what someone else says, they turn the conversation back to themselves and take off with a new story.

When talking with a Performer, the central factor to realize is how they enjoy the stage. The strategy is to grant them this and move on. "Now that we've heard your story, let's hear from someone else."

If you are a performer and want to experiment with migrating to other styles, consider deliberately imitating your opposite, the Nurturer. Before you try it yourself, you may want to observe a really skilled listener and watch how they do it.

Then make a commitment to yourself to try, for some limited period of time, to focus purely on someone else, to listen, reflect, probe, seek 100% to understand and not to talk about yourself. You'll be amazed at the satisfaction that can come from listening.

The Explorer

The Explorer has potentially the easiest path to fully actualized Mindful Conversations, but that does not guarantee success nor make it a straight shot. The Explorer often tilts toward the speaking role, like the Performer, but because her style is balanced by a strong pull towards nurturing also, she is typically not as extreme as the Performer. If she is aware of her own and other's needs, the Explorer can balance all four styles and bring enormous value to the conversation.

The Explorer asks herself the question, "Are we achieving our purpose? How can I help us be successful?" She is looking at the big picture and working for the interests of the whole. She is often a leader, willing and able to guide a conversation or group to make sure that its goals (stated or assumed) are met. The explorer is thus often able to help the whole group (be that two people, five or fifty) achieve greater satisfaction by playing a facilitator role. She is able to become a temporary nurturer, drawing out the quiet member, "Frank, you look thoughtful but we haven't heard from you..." as well as moderating a dominator, "Thank you, Arial. Sounds like you had an exciting time on your trip. I'm wondering who else might have had a related experience."

You can recognize an Explorer by her ability to talk openly and seemingly unselfconsciously for a time, and then to revert to a more reflective mode, to draw others out and to take in different points of view. She may not be the best entertainer in the group, nor perhaps the most insightful, nor even the most supportive, but the Explorer's flexibility and openness to the dance makes her welcome in any group or conversation.

The Explorer's strength can become a weakness if she allows herself to be pulled into too many directions, or takes on too much responsibility for managing the group and the conversation. Working overtime to manage all the dynamics can become a mask that can actually conceal the Explorer's own deeper personal needs.

The Explorer's growth path may be to let go of some of the responsibilities she feels, create space and invite others to assume leadership responsibilities. In this way, she can be more free to inhabit (for a time) one of the other styles or roles.

Introverts and Extroverts

The larger picture that the Conversation Style Guide taps into is the bias that we all have toward extroversion or introversion. One of the most destructive cultural myths currently propagated in so many ways is the suggestion that extroversion is somehow better. I hope that this assessment (and this book) will be a step toward debunking that unfortunate and untrue myth. The message of Mindful Conversation is that conversation is a dance, not a competition. Success and satisfaction are derived from authenticity, not from any degree of extroversion or introversion. We don't need more extroverts; we don't need more introverts. We need you. Further focus on this cultural dynamic is beyond the scope of this book. But for one who grew up as a dedicated introvert, I must again add a word about the pain of this dominant myth. I suffered, deeply, for years trying to fit in by trying to act like an extrovert. It didn't work for me, and it's highly unlikely to work for you. The irony, and delight, for me, however has been how strikingly the fact of accepting my introversion awakened my extroverted recessive style, to the point that I now consistently score myself as an Explorer.

Notes from the Journey

Core Awareness: Conversations consists of listening, reflecting and speaking. We all have a style that favors listening/reflecting or speaking, and it is often either "me" focused or "other" focused.

Core Values: Authenticity involves being aware of and true to our natural bias, but also recognizing that we have the ability to go beyond our comfort zone, act beyond our bias.

Core Skill: The ability to notice our biases and choose different conversational styles to serve different intentions and situations.

Core Tool: The Conversational Style Assessment can guide you in directions you want to pursue to expand your range of effective conversation.

Next Steps

Get started by taking the Conversational Style Assessment, at:

https://www.survey.alchemer.com/s3/5989413/
4d7074977c7e

You will receive a customized report, describing your conversational style, its strengths and limitations, and ways that you might work to expand your repertoire, if you so desire.

Chapter 4
Begin at the Beginning

"Can we say 'Hello' again, Harvey. I'm practicing my beginnings."

If you sometimes wonder how to start a conversation, you're not alone. In the next three chapters, we'll unravel the basic phases of any conversation: beginning, middle, and end. Each phase has a purpose and a few principles. Understanding the basics can give you confidence to navigate the territory without getting lost.

Most of us give little thought to how we begin conversations. Beginning a conversation is all about **Connection.** Skip the foreplay, and you may end up with a disappointing main event.

The middle of the conversation is about exploration and

discovery. Conversation is a dance, not a march. You may have some idea of what will happen, but you can't know in advance. Anything can happen. And often does. Stay open to discovery.

The ending is about closure. Whether the conversation has lasted 30 seconds or 3 hours, if it has been of worth, then it is appropriate to bring it to an end with some acknowledgment of what has happened.

Jumping In ...
Establishing Connection

Who hasn't stood on the threshold of wanting to start a conversation, only to go weak in the knees, soft in the head, dry in the mouth and stuck in the tongue? "Threshold paralysis" a friend calls it. This chapter will help you leap over this self- created obstacle and be ready to soar.

What should I say? Do I dare? Once you understand how simple it is to start, what fun, and what a gift, instead of the dare question, you'll be like a kid at the edge of the pool on opening day. Maybe a slight twinge of nervousness, but overall so ready to be in that water. Think back to recent conversations you've had. Very likely, you barely remember the words that were spoken. What you probably do remember is the experience. How you felt. Comfortable? Awkward? Free to express yourself? Understood? It's all about connection. You remember presence, far more than content.

Connection is Job #1. Connect with yourself and connect with your CP. Not too many people think of welcoming themselves, but it's a great place to start.

Welcome yourself by taking a breath. Do whatever helps you to be present in the moment and in your body, as much as possible without judgment and without manipulative motivation. "Here I am. Ahh." Setting an intention for the conversation can be an excellent place to start. This may be fully intuitive for a spontaneous chat, or it may require some conscious planning for a longer or more difficult conversation. How do you want to show up? A few words, a mini pep talk.

"Get to know Martha." "Just be together, as friends." "Listen to Jack's recent experience." Even before the topics you might talk about, what is the tone you want to project?

Connection is a feeling. It has nothing to do with content (*what* you are going to talk about). Connection is about an inner experience: *you are someone I want to share myself with.* Connection is not rational, not even cerebral. Just a feeling. A matter of the heart, not the brain. An all-important feeling that paves the way for a satisfying, open conversation. Signal an open, friendly approach with a smile, a nod, eye contact, a handshake, a wink or a hug, whatever is appropriate in the relationship and circumstance.

These are the tools of welcome. Many of us feel shy around strangers or even when first meeting friends. Help your CP feel comfortable. This will in turn diminish your own discomfort. "A stranger is a friend in disguise."

A genuine, warm moment of connection will get you and your CP off to the right start. A waltz always has three steps. To start your dance, try these:

1. Make eye contact
2. Smile and include any appropriate physical gesture
3. Learn (if necessary) and use your CP's name

Use these simple steps to minimize any lingering fears and to establish connection, whether your CP is an old or new friend. Note that #1 and #2 are both nonverbal. The most powerful tools for connection are often non-verbal. It's a feeling. If you're not in the habit of making eye contact when you greet others, this will take practice.

If a real smile lies within you, share it. Not a toothpaste smile, but something that says, "I'm happy to be alive. I'm happy you're alive. Let's connect."

For extra credit, add in some kind of *appropriate* physical gesture. Some people welcome hugs and kisses, but never presume. A slight touch on the arm can do it, a handshake, or even just a brief hand gesture – no actual touch but the suggestion. Be sensitive to culture, gender and other norms.

Never force any kind of physical contact. If you pick up any resistance, back off immediately. This can all happen in a second or two. The on ramp to connection is primarily non-verbal.

We all have a name, and most of us like to hear it spoken.

It validates us, and draws us a little deeper into the conversation. Along with the smile, it says, "You are worth knowing." If you know your CP's name, use it. If you don't know or have forgotten, ask, and then use it. Speaking the name will help reinforce it in your memory. If you forget a name later in the conversation, swallow your embarrassment and ask again. Make a joke or game out of it, or even turn it into a discussion. I use an apology such as, "I'm embarrassed, I've forgotten your name already. And, by the way, I'm Peter, in case you've forgotten mine. Do you have as much trouble with names as I do? I'm trying to work on remembering." Note how this leads you potentially into a common activity (improving name recall), allows you to expose a minor vulner-ability (memory), and puts you on the same team against a common problem (forgetting names). Not bad for openers. Net result: you'll probably remember their name and likely they'll remember yours.

Reinforce remembering your CP's name by using it at least once again in the conversation. Not in every sentence. That feels sleazy to me, but sprinkle it in.

If this seems childish to you, I say, "Fine, bring out the inner child. Play. Have fun with it." (See Chapter 14 for more detailed discussion of play and humor in conversation.) The more fun you can make this, the more likely you are to continue. Make this beginning conscious, welcoming and open. A simple start and you're on your way.

Obviously the opening is different with someone you know or a stranger, and different between someone you know very well vs. a casual acquaintance, but the principle is the same: Connect first, then converse. Make this person, with whom you are about to share yourself, feel like they are the most important person in the room. Because they are. They are the one you are with at this time and this place. Here and now, the present, the moment that matters.

If the above is foreign to you or sounds difficult, practice the basic moves, perhaps in front of a mirror. Write reflections in your conversational journal and/or practice with a partner whom you know and trust. Reward yourself if you remain mindful and follow these simple steps. One time earns a piece of chocolate, three in a row is an ice cream. Whatever reminds you that you have made a significant step forward.

An introduction to Small Talk

Most conversations begin with a few words of banter, aka "small talk." It's fashionable to dismiss small talk, but if you want to swim in the ocean, first you must wade through the surf. Small talk is nothing to be ashamed about (unless you never move beyond it). Small talk is more about listening, than it is about speaking.

Good small talk gets both parties involved and gives clues for possible fruitful deeper conversation.

I had a doctor's appointment this afternoon. The receptionist who took me in, first came across to me as brusque and uninterested. Maybe having a bad day, or who knows? She took my vitals. We were like two stones that ended up in the same ditch. I was as distant to her as she to me.

Then I decided it was time for a Mindful Re-launch. I looked at her, really looked at her for the first time. I noticed her shoes and socks. Her red, black and white socks had large polka dots bouncing all over; her shoes were beyond lovely. I inquired. She lit up. We talked shoes, then fashion, and then dancing. Two minutes maybe. She smiled. I smiled. I felt my heart opening up. By the time she had finished my vitals, I was genuinely sorry to see her go. Curiosity, one little question, that's all it took.

Here are my top ten guidelines for small talk openers. Try any that appeal. Better yet, write your own.

TEN PRINCIPLES FOR PRODUCTIVE, OPENING SMALL TALK [8]

1. Have fun with it. Be light. Don't try to score points, impress, or dominate. Avoid confrontation or long stories.

2. Dial up your authentic curiosity. Enquire and listen for "free information," any fact, opinion, article of clothing, or feeling that you genuinely want to follow up on. If someone says, "I'm going to a movie tonight," that's an invitation for an inquiry. "What kind of movies do you like? What's the best movie you've seen recently?" Clues are everywhere. Watch and listen for them. Show interest. Ask questions. For a profound exploration of this topic alone, see Will Wise's *Ask Powerful Questions*. Curiosity is the gateway to connection.

3. Compliment, sincerely and directly. Follow with an exploratory question, e.g., "I love those socks. Where could I

find some like that?" If complimented yourself, take it in, respond with a smile and a genuine "thank you" and move on (unless you genuinely want to explore the area of the compliment as a topic of conversation).

4. Look for ways to help. "Looks like you need an extra hand. Can I hold that plate for you? Can I get you a drink?" Conversely, ask for help if you need it. Both giving and receiving help you engage with your CP. "I'm looking for a good restaurant in the area. Can you suggest one?"

5. Seek and explore any overlapping activity or interest. "We're both tall (or short, or ...) ... Do you come here often? ... You look like someone who enjoys the out-of-doors ... What is your connection to this organization / topic / host / gathering?" Be ever alert for shared interests and common ground.

6. Share some easy point of self-disclosure or vulnerability. "This is such a huge group. I'm more comfortable in smaller gatherings." This is taking a small risk, but sharing your own vulnerability is a great way to build trust. "It's been a long day for me. Stressful at work. How about you?" (Sharing a vulnerability and seeking common ground.)

7. Prepare your own list of easy, small talk topics. For example, if you're going to a party, an easy opener is, "How do you know the host?" The weather, trite as it can be, presents interesting opportunities, especially if you go beyond the norm. Instead of, "Hot enough for you?" try something like, "Phew, hot isn't it. What's your favorite way to stay cool in hot weather?"

8. Basic biography is a great opener. Everyone has a back-story, and most people are happy to share it. Where did you grow up? Do you come from a large or small family?

(One question like this can open a world.) Have you lived here for long? Did you attend school locally?

9. Combine a short, personal story with a related inquiry. For example, "Something special happened to me today. I got a phone call from a friend I haven't heard from in several years. We had such a nice visit, made my day. Anything special happen to you today?" If your CP mentions that she likes to garden, use this as an opportunity for brief self-disclosure and a specific inquiry, such as, "I'd love to have a vegetable garden, but I've never had much success. What do you grow in your garden?"

10. Avoid difficult or the cliché questions, such as "How's life?" or "Tell me about yourself." Many people feel lost in the face of such broad openers. Make your inquiries open-ended but focused, e.g., "I'd love to hear more about your trip." "What do you like to do in your spare time?" "What part of your job is most challenging / difficult / enjoyable for you?" See how much you can learn about someone, as if you were going to write about them.

If you're interested in a list of potential opening questions, then I suggest you browse the internet:

https://conversationstartersworld.com/
250-conversation- starters/#books

There's enough material there to keep you busy for years.

Another good source to help get beyond the awkward-ness is

https://www.rd.com/advice/relationships/
conversation-skills/

Follow the guidelines above to leap across threshold paralysis and launch a mindful conversation. Your conversational partners, like you, want to connect. As you begin a new conversation, be aware that this moment has never happened before and never will again. The Self that is you, the smiles that you spread, the hope in your heart, the words, the gestures, the stories, the jokes, the understandings — open this window into another's world. Surrender to the moment, and it is yours.

Notes from the Journey

Core Awareness: Establish a connection in the first few seconds of a conversation with 3 simple tools:

1. Eye contact

2. Smile and appropriate physical gesture.

3. Use of your CP's name.

Core Value: Curiosity. And it must be authentic. Open yourself to being and expressing your curiosity about others. Seek to understand and learn about your CP.

Core Skill: Acknowledging your fears or blocks and moving beyond them, embracing possibility.

Core Tools: Eye Contact. Smile. Physical gesture. Learn and use the name.

Next Steps

1. Learn and use the name. This requires focus. Set yourself a goal, for example, if you're at a party, to ask and learn 3 new names. You can practice in stores, at church, in a class, bar or wherever. Listen when you first ask, then use the name immediately after you learn it. "Great to meet you, Paula." Think about the name as you say it. Commit to use the name at least twice, once at the beginning and once at the end of the conversation. "I enjoyed talking with you, Paula."

2. When first meeting someone, do a quick scan for some item that awakens your curiosity and inquire about it. Use the item to open a deeper conversation. Possibilities are limitless. For example, "What an unusual ring. I bet there's a story behind that?" Who knows where a simple remark like that might lead? If you're open.

Chapter 5

Merge with the Magic in the Middle

"Perhaps if I got to know you ... but there is something slightly off-putting about your manner."

You're in it now, the magic in the middle. Anything can, and often does, happen. Imagine the possible. Live the joy Time to jump in.

Explore.

Mindful Conversations are like a symphony, swelling and

lulling, striking off in new directions, returning to earlier themes, evolving, growing, reprising. You are composer, conductor, player, and audience. You pass the lead back and forth between yourself and your CP's. You listen. You speak. Take in the music you are making. Enjoy it. Give it all you've got.

What and How

A fundamental distinction in all conversation is between "What" you are talking about and "How" you are talking.

Content and Process. In conversation, the "what" is the topic. The "how" is the means of discussion. In Mindful Conversation, there are really only three "meta-moves" you can be engaged in. At any one time, you can be listening (covered in Part 2); speaking (covered in Part 3) or pausing to reflect (Chapter 11).

Listening and speaking each have many sub-processes.

When listening, you may be silent. You could be mirroring back what you hear. You could be asking questions. You also may be not listening at all, but actually thinking about what you'll be doing tomorrow. Or what you did yesterday. Each of these will enormously impact the conversation. If speaking, you could be telling a story, thinking out loud, or outlining an argument, confronting or collaborating with your CP's.

Most people are not particularly aware of the process, the tone, the non-verbal messages they are using. Such processes are like the air you breathe. They can sustain you or kill you. Worth your attention.

Much of the rest of this book is about strategies, attitudes, and tools that will help you navigate this magic territory in the middle. This chapter will stay at a high level with master strategies, broad principles for any conversation. Parts 2 and 3 dive into details.

Three Guidelines

Whether you are speaking or listening, there are 3 over-arching, process guidelines that will help you to create more Mindful Conversation.

1. Share Air Time

2. Seek Fertile Ground

3. Seize the Moment

1. SHARE AIR TIME

"Parity" is the roughly equal sharing of time between speaking and listening. This is not possible or even desirable in every conversation. The question to ask yourself is more global. Overall, do you tend to participate fully, sometimes as a speaker and sometimes as a listener? Speaking, both professionally or socially, means revealing something about yourself (an experience or story, a thought or opinion, a wish, a problem, a feeling etc.). Listening means taking in information, also attending to, drawing out, and understanding your CP's.

The word "conversation" implies that you're in this *with* your CP's. Your behavior supports one another. Ideally no one dominates. No one hides.

As explored in Chapter 3, we all have conversational biases. Some of us are more comfortable speaking and some listening. With certain topics, you are more familiar and may do more speaking, others where you are more naturally the listener.[9]

You can't control how others are going to conduct themselves. All the more reason for managing yourself, being clear on your intention, and modeling behaviors that bring out the best in you and (hopefully) your CP's.

I was recently at a party and ended up talking with Debby, previously a stranger. Debby said she was a writer. I was, of course, interested. Until she launched into a detailed plot description of her book, scene by scene. My eyes glazed over, but she was just warming up. When she indicated that there would be a sequel, I made a quick exit.

Who hasn't been marooned with a Dominating Debby?

Most of us run, or want to run away, but perhaps don't dare. Most Dominant Debbies are oblivious of their impact. As long as you'll listen, they'll talk. But you do have a choice.

I don't want to be rude, but neither do I want to be bored. I usually listen for a while, then try to interject something and see what happens. If there is no reciprocity, my brain tunes out. So I plan my exit.

If you're hopelessly stuck with a Dominant Debbie, here are a couple of quirky, but effective strategies. These were pioneered by Sara, a generally shy woman and a coaching client of mine. They take a bit of courage, but what's to lose? The first is simply to raise your hand, high, and hold it there until you're called on. Just like in school. I love this strategy. It's non-verbal, clear but non-confrontational, and hard to ignore. A second, somewhat higher level of intervention, is to put your hands on Dominant Debbie's shoulders and look her in the eye. When she stops talking (which she will), say in a strong but non- threatening voice, "I have something I'd like to say, too."

The opposite of Dominant Debbie is Silent Sam, who cloaks himself in silence, revealing little of himself. When I'm in conversation, I want someone to push up against, someone with substance of their own to share. I am stimulated, challenged, and enlightened by others' experiences. It's more fun to dance with another, than by myself.

If someone doesn't want to talk, or is uncomfortable, you

can't force it. There are many ways to communicate that you are ready and eager to hear what they have to say – if they are willing to speak. Section 2 covers a host of such tools.

If you have a strong Debbie in you, try practicing deliberately to be an Observer (see Chapter 3) for a while. Set yourself a goal to draw someone else out through questions and reflective listening. If you're more of a Silent Sam, begin experimenting with your inner Performer. Set a goal to introduce a topic of your choosing. Select a subject that you care about, or know about, or want to learn about. Challenge yourself to learn and grow through your conversation. Reward yourself when you take a chance. You deserve it.

Create parity, a basic principle of Mindful Conversation.

2. SEEK FERTILE GROUND

There are two ways to discover fertile ground for your conversations: (A) Speak about what matters to you and (B) be curious about others.

A. Speak About What Matters to You

Too many conversations smell like last week's trash. Same old stories, same tired jokes, no challenge, no growth. Mindful conversations are new and fresh, journeys of discovery and exploration. A vital step is to consider what you really want to talk about, and be willing to share your experience openly. Put the issue and yourself on the table. If you're inspired by the movie you just saw, or consumed by your troubled relationship, or puzzled by your psychotic cat, any of these can become the focus for a Mindful Conversation. Find a way to move beyond your initial fear or resistance to change.

If, for example, you're going to be in a group, make a list (preferably in writing) of topics that you'd like to engage around and opening remarks or questions for each. Think of 3 - 5 topics that interest you that you could explore, and at least two opening comments or questions for each. For example, a random list could look something like this:

Topic	Opening Comments or Questions
1. Books and Movies	1. Read any good books recently? Any good movies? 2. I'm reading a book now that I just love, Xxx. I wonder if you know it?
2. Gardening	1. Are you a gardener? Ready for Spring? 2. Do you know a good arborist? I need some help with a tree on my property.
3. Technology	1. We're wrestling with limiting our kids' use of technology. Have you had to confront that issue? 2. I get so frustrated with passwords being rejected. Do you have that problem? I've found a couple of great apps to help me keep track.

Here is a short list of universal topics. Exercise your question muscle. For each topic, write one question that goes beyond the most typical cliché.

- o Work (yours, mine, work/life balance)
- o Hobbies (yours, mine, trends)
- o Food (cooking, restaurants, healthy, diets)
- o Clothes (style, favorites, where to buy)
- o Families / Parenting (Family rituals, family backgrounds, parenting joys and challenges)
- o Entertainment (Music, Books, Music, TV ...)

o   Sports (Participating, Watching)

o   Health (Healthy habits, Diet, Stress)

o   State of the world. State of the Nation / State / Local (News Sources, Top stories, Society, Hopes, Worries)

o   Nature (Environment, Favorite spots)

o   Pets (Cats, Dogs, Unusual pets)

There are thousands of possibilities. Search the internet; you'll find many lists, but the best list is the one you create for yourself. Again, it's a chance to exercise your curiosity muscle.

Another source of topics for inquiry is anything that your CP mentions, even in passing. Say you're talking with someone who says, "I passed you on the street the other day as I was heading to class." Many will respond to such a comment with an "Oh" or an immediate grabbing response, "Oh, yes, I was going to the grocery store." Such responses completely miss the opportunity created by the mention of a class:

o   What class are you taking?

o   Why are you taking this class? What do you hope to get out of it?

o   What are you learning about X?

o   What do you like about the class? Not like?

o   Is the class large/small? Challenging? Easy?

Any one of these could initiate a Mindful Conversation. And there is the always applicable question, "How interesting. Tell me more about X?"

Your topics will change as your interests, problems or priorities alter. The key point is to be ready to focus the conversation on what's interesting vs the same tired stuff that doesn't excite or challenge you.

Some recoil at the idea of planning a conversation in advance. A conversation should be spontaneous, they say. I say that planning and spontaneity are not mutually exclusive. Open yourself to the experience, and you can be spontaneous about a subject you've identified and prepared for in advance. I plan for what I'd like, expect the unexpected, and embrace what shows up. Conversation is a living organism that deserves my best self. I come prepared.

The choice of topic and how you present is influenced by how personally open or revealing you are willing to be. Suppose you want to talk about your cat, who has been acting strange recently. You can be very direct ("My cat, Romeo, has PTSD, I think. Are you a cat person?") or slide the subject into the conversation ("Cats are such interesting animals, don't you think?") An effective introduction is often a combination of personal statement and question. "I'm worried about my cat, Romeo. He doesn't seem himself. Have you had any experience with a cat with PTSD?" Note that all 3 of these examples explicitly invite the CP into the conversation.

B. Be Curious about Others

A second master strategy for finding fertile ground is to be curious about others, aka "Get people to talk about themselves." This profound principle is remarkably rare in conversation. Most people spend 60% - 80% of their conversational time talking about themselves. That's not a typo. MRI studies at Harvard's Neuroscience Lab[10] indicate that the pleasure centers in the brain most associated with self- disclosure are linked to motivational states also associated with sex, drugs and good food. Learn to defer the instant gratification that comes from talking about yourself. The rewards will come

75

many times over, counted by the friends and connections you will make, who will now *want* to hear about you instead of dreading it.

Being curious about others is such a simple connecting strategy, but many people NEVER inquire. Their only means of response is a grabbing one. Tell them a story about your summer vacation, and their only modes of response are the blank stare or, "I went to X for my vacation." Practice inquiry.

Practice reflective responses. Go beneath the facts. Experiment with openers like "Why? What? How? Tell me about ... I'd love to know more about ..." Part 2 of this book will give you more specific details.

3. SEIZE THE MOMENT

The third principle is being aware and present to the magic of the moment. If you are aware of yourself and willing to be authentic, which means being willing to be vulnerable, then your conversation may not always be neat and orderly, but it will be engaging, and it can be magical. When you are vulnerable, others are more likely to be also. It's the ticket to connection. Together, you can dance the night away in the ballroom of our common humanity.

As an introvert, I shied away from this principle for years. I remember one particular dinner party. I'd been pretty quiet, resting in my default observer role. As I surveyed the rest of the party, I noticed Milly's new eyeglasses. They looked great on her. As a lifetime eyeglasses wearer, a world of stories and questions opened in front of me like a magic fountain. The conversation spread to others, and we spent the next twenty minutes discussing the role of eyeglasses in our lives, where to get them, how they've affected us. We got into public and private images, what images we want to project and what images we actually do project. The conversation stretched out in so many directions. Good fun, spontaneous, without plan or purpose – except to express and connect. That's mindful conversation.

Small children are masters at this, but too often, we lose the spark of authenticity as we "mature." We morph into tired actors trained to speak our lines, struggling to fill time and space, rather than really engaging in exploration. The fertile territory is often buried beneath the surface, not in the script but in the heart, hidden not by the curtain but by the fear of being seen or appearing strange. Be ready to toss the script and follow the heart. Mindful conversation includes conscious planning for sure, but is often more about improvisation than performance.

What if I don't want to engage?

Every conversation is an invitation, but not an obligation, to engage. If you don't want to, or don't have time to, or are too preoccupied in the moment to be present, its best to declare yourself and move on. Authenticity (the second value of the C.A.R.E. Model) requires this. More attending, less pretending.

Cutting off a conversation (maybe before it has even started) can feel awkward. The trick is to be both respectful and direct. Learn how to tell someone that you are not available for conversation right now. Circumstances, the relationship and your personal style will determine the details. The following are sample words to consider and adapt to your style.

- o "I'd like to talk, but I have to leave. I'm sorry but I don't have time right now." Or "I have only ten minutes. Can we talk for ten?" (Or, "Could we talk later?")

- o "I have an appointment I must leave for. I'm sorry. Will you please excuse me?"

- o "I've enjoyed talking with you about X. I need to ... if you'll excuse me."

These statements have two critical elements in common: they state your position clearly, and, when possible, explain the reason. Many people will immediately consider such open, direct statements difficult, or even rude. But consider, which is more rude, to acknowledge whatever conversation you've had and tell someone honestly that you're not available to continue, or to pretend to listen while you're actually plotting your exit strategy?

Be direct. Be respectful. Move on.

Notes from the Journey

Core Awareness: 3 principles:

1. Share Air Time

2. Seek Fertile Ground

3. Seize the Moment

Core Value: The C.A.R.E. Model (Curiosity, Authenticity, Respect and Empathy).

Core Skill: Carrying your intention forward into action. Staying calm and true to yourself.

Core Tools: Dare to be vulnerable. Take a reasonable risk.

Next Steps

1. There is so much to practice here. Don't let it overwhelm you. Choose one of the 3 guidelines. In your journal, write about what this means to you, and why it's important. Make an index card that celebrates this principle, and carry it with you for one week. Hold it in your mind before important conversations. Write in your journal any reflections on the impact of focusing on that principle.

2. Make a table with 3 - 5 topics, including possible opening comments or questions that you'd like to explore in conversation in the next week. Institute at least one such conversation.

Chapter 6
End When it's Over

Ever been in a conversation that ends abruptly when you realize your CP has gone missing? I have. I felt abandoned and foolish. Many conversations end when one person or the other ... just ... drifts ... away. Perhaps someone more inviting waltzed by. You're left wondering. *What happened? Did I say something wrong?*

A Closing Ceremony

Often you realize (from tone, mood, non-verbal signs, the time, etc.) that you're reaching the end of the conversation. Someone makes little closing motions. Standing or putting on the coat and gloves is a sure sign.

Closing properly is like putting the lid on the jar before it goes back on the shelf. It frees you to move on. A good closing acknowledges what has passed between you and your CP. It's a way of saying, "Thank you" for the gift of your time and attention. Close properly and you are far more likely to be remembered...and welcomed back!

This doesn't have to be a big deal. "Thanks for the chat," may be all that's required. But if the conversation has been special for you in any way, then a small ceremony may be in order.

Here are the four basic tools that I advocate:

1. Eye contact and appropriate touch.

2. Name use

3. Summarize and acknowledge something from the conversation that stood out for you.

4. Suggest a next step if appropriate (and if you'd like there to be one).

Closing often happens fast, so don't hesitate and lose the opportunity. Make eye contact and, (if appropriate) touch or gesture. Sound familiar? Parallel to how we started. Start with connection and end with connection. As for the gesture, a parting hug may feel right. A handshake can do it. Under other circumstances, a wave, or slight suggestion of touch even if there is no physical contact. As in the opening (Chapter 4), use the name. Even in conversations where you never exchanged names, it's not too late. "I'm sorry. I never got your name ... Well, thank you, Sally. Pleasure talking to you." Take a second to reinforce what we all long for – to be seen and acknowledged.

Summarizing some special topic or moment of meaning is desirable, not always possible. It's the bow on the package.

"Sandy, I so enjoyed hearing about your trip to Cuba. I hope I can go some day." That takes five seconds. It marks the moment, makes it more memorable. If something feels unresolved or unfinished, this is a good time to mention it. "I know there isn't time now, but I still have questions about the project. I'd like to talk about it again." Whatever you say, be authentic and affirming. Establish eye contact, and speak what you mean.

Suggest a next step – if you'd like there to be one. "If you're in town again, I'd welcome another visit" or whatever seems appropriate. If it's not appropriate or you don't want to see this person again, then obviously, skip this step. But if you would like there to be a next step, then I urge you to suggest something reasonably easy and appropriate to the conversation and the relationship. The easiest one is "I hope we meet again." Being more specific creates a better likelihood of it happening. If you don't get an instantaneous yes, try not to take it personally. Let it go, and move on.

How to Exit a Burning Building ... Gracefully

The above ending scenarios are straightforward in an ideal world, but the world is often not ideal. Perhaps the conversation didn't go so well. You were rushed or stressed. Perhaps you suspect that your CP didn't hear a word you said. Perhaps you didn't enjoy the time, and were eager to leave.

Here is a list of exit strategies that can help you escape, quickly but respectfully.

1. Short and sweet. "Thank you, for the chance to catch up (talk about the family etc.) Mere use of the words, "Thank you" can bring even a difficult

conversation to a more mutually satisfying close (so long as you do feel thankful for some part of what transpired between you).

2. Networker's favorite: "Will you excuse me? I promised myself I'd circulate about. Thank you for the conversation."

3. Little white lies. "Please excuse me. I promised to call home (help with the dishes, check on the game, get the laundry ...).

4. Pass them off. "Oh, here's my friend, Joe. Let me introduce you."

5. Gotta go. "Can you tell me where the rest room is?"

6. I need a drink (bite to eat, etc.) Can I get you something before I go?"

7. Mission accomplished. "Well thanks for the advice about where to look for shoes."

Notes from the Journey

Core Awareness: You are about to transition out of the conversation. Mark the moment.

Core Value: Respect. By taking a moment to acknowledge the ending, you show respect for your CP and the time he's given to the conversation.

Core Skill: Focus and intention. This is a relatively straightforward assignment. It requires intention and attention.

Core Tools: Eye contact, use of name, touch or gesture.

Next Steps

1. By definition, you will have as many opportunities to practice endings as you have conversations. Establish the intention to make your endings matter. Wrap the package, then tie the bow. The minimum is name use and "Thank you."

Section 1
My Summary and Action Plan

Take a moment to scan over what you've read and jot down your reflections.

1. My Points of Awareness / Insights:

2. My Potential Implementation Challenges:

3. My Action Plan:

Part 2

The External Conversation

Chapter 7
Listen, Please

"I only interrupt when I have something more important to say. ...
And now I need to get on with my life."

Mindful listening is the heart of the Mindful Conversation. Skillful, intentional listening is your best possible on ramp to understanding and connection. This too often ignored practice can transform you into a powerful, effective, sought after, and joyous communicator. Without this skill, even if you are articulate, knowledgeable and wise, you are as handicapped as a one-legged sprinter.

My wife Wendy was car-pooling home from an excursion. Riding in the passenger seat, she struck up a conversation with Adam, the driver, whom she'd never met before. After she inquired and learned that he designed and made wooden toys for tots, she engaged him on the topic. The conversation flowed naturally to his children, his family, and his growing up years.

After the trip, Ginger, who had been eavesdropping from the back seat, immediately commandeered Wendy off to one side.

"How did you do that?" Ginger inquired. Wendy was puzzled. "Do what?"

"I've known Adam forever. You learned more about him in one 45-minute drive than I have in 25 years." Ginger paused, fixed Wendy in her gaze. "I need to know how you did that."

When Wendy told me that story over dinner, I repeated Ginger's question, "How *did* you do it?"

"I was curious," she said. "I asked questions. He seemed eager to talk. I was ready to listen."

Curiosity

Compare two different starts to Wendy and Adam's conversation:

Scenario A

Wendy: So, what kind of work do you do?

Adam: I design and make wooden toys for children.

Wendy: I have a five-year-old granddaughter. I gave her a set of blocks. I don't like all the plastic stuff. I remember a favorite toy I had ..."

Scenario B

Wendy: So, what kind of work do you do?

Adam: I design and make wooden toys for children.

Wendy: Designing and making toys, what a delightful way to

make a living. How did you get started on that? Is it as much fun as it sounds?

You can imagine how differently the conversation is likely to evolve from Scenario B (Reflective Response) vs Scenario A (Grabbing Response)? Which is the more common type of response? Which is likely to take the conversation deeper? Scenario B is an inquiry, Wendy demonstrating interest in Adam and what he has said. Adam and Wendy quickly become conversational co-explorers, walking down a path of discovery together. Scenario A sets them up as competitors, two talkers each clawing away to own the conversation, voices interested mostly in themselves.

The first of the four values of Mindful Conversation is curiosity. Wendy's response in Scenario B is the flowering of curiosity. Hers were questions that anyone could ask. They were non-threatening, open-ended, and inviting. Curiosity lies at the heart of mindful listening.

When you follow your curiosity and listen mindfully, you can be an effective conversational partner with anyone, at any time, about any topic.

Basic Facts

Mindful Listening accomplishes two distinct and vital goals:

1. It helps you to understand, and therefore to connect with your CP.

2. It gives your CP the affirming and deeply satisfying experience of having been listened to, and thereby builds relationship.

In so many conversations, neither of these conditions are met. In fact, many people have *never* been deeply listened to.

And many of these same people have never really listened to anyone else. They're too involved in "trying to grab the ball" to consider sharing it.

Mindful listening starts with intention. You will hear what you are listening for. Who are you, as you listen? Are you listening to understand? To probe? To judge? To diagnose? To compete? Set a clear *intention* for your conversation.

Mindful listening is not a difficult skill to understand, but it takes patience and practice to develop into a habit. It is often blocked by competing habits and desires such as judgment, discomfort around or no experience with the language of feelings, or an ego that can't let go of the need to dominate the conversation.

Three Styles of Listening

Listening lives along a continuum: from non-listening, to light listening, to deep listening. We'll explore Deep Listening in Chapter 8, but first:

1. NON-LISTENING

"Non-listening" isn't even a type of listening, but I include it because it is unfortunately *the most common* listening style.

Non-listeners are often consumed by distractions or awash in self-absorbed anxiety. They are, for any one of many reasons, unavailable. They may be drowning in the desire to impress, please, or entertain, their ears clogged to any voice other than their own. Perpetual non-listeners are like a camera only able to take selfies. They frequently interrupt, finish other people's sentences, talk over others, or tune-out entirely, barely biding their time until they can speak. The non-listener rarely asks questions or expends any energy in trying to understand what another is saying.

Non-listeners are not bad people. Most are just unconscious and / or unskilled. If you find yourself frequently in a non-listening mode, as we all do at times, I suggest you ask yourself a basic question: "What is my listening intention? Am I able / do I want to engage with X right now?"

If you don't want to or are not able to engage, then extricate yourself (except in emergency situations) from the conversation, as honestly but respectfully as possible. (See suggestions for how to do this, later in this chapter.) If your answer is, "Yes, I'd like to engage with X," then set your intention to good listening. Take a moment to calm yourself and breathe, consciously. No one will notice. It is like a momentary meditation. Consider "What about this person or topic interests me? What would make this conversation engaging?" Or try any of the reflective responses discussed later in this chapter. The essence of good listening, your intention, is to communicate to your partner that you are interested in what they are saying, how they are thinking or feeling, and who they are. The trick is to move from being a non-listener to being actively involved in drawing out and understanding your CP.

Don't worry. You'll get your chance to speak too. But first, demonstrate interest in your CP. Focus your attention on understanding. It's a game changer.

2. LIGHT LISTENING

On a rainy walk recently, I ran into a neighbor I know slightly, but hadn't seen in some time. We stopped, spent five minutes chatting about the weather and the implications of the forest fires we'd been experiencing, then moved on. I listened to her. She listened to me. The talk tacitly acknowledged our commonality: neighbors sharing a common worry. It was small talk. But small talk can also be joyous, worthwhile talk. I felt happy for it, connected in a delightful, unentangled way. I returned home, refreshed, unburdened, a member of a loose tribe, ready for the day. I think she felt something similar.

Light Listening is a huge improvement over non-listening.

The light listener recognizes that conversation is a give and take, trading off speaking and listening. The unspoken message from the light listener is *You are worthy of my time and attention. We will meet in this moment, enjoy one another, and then move on.* The light listener listens to the words, asks appropriate questions when they occur, and shares her own stories and ideas. You and your CP are popcorn popping, briefly, together.

Light listening can and should be fun, hopeful, helpful and supportive. It meets a lot of our needs.

The Joys of Light Listening

On a daily basis, most of us have multiple opportunities for healthy, enjoyable light listening. A short exchange with the barista in the coffee shop or the customer service rep on the telephone is an opportunity. Giving value and importance to these small moments of connection is fulfilling. Seize the moment. Repeatedly I find that light listening turns a task that I might resist, or merely tolerate, into a moment where I feel more alive and thriving. Such moments put an extra bounce in my day.

To create joyful light listening moments, we move from "It-It" to mindful "Me-You" conversation. An "It-It" [11] moment is one in which a person in some role (a client, a buyer, an information seeker, even a friend) bumps up against another (a salesman, a bank teller, a colleague, etc.). In "It-It" moments, we relate to the other, not as a person, but as a function. (For an example, see my story of the visit to the doctor, in Chapter 4.) A "Me-You" moment, by contrast, is when two or more sentient human beings share one another's presence for a time, acknowledging that they are, after all, united as one, part of a common life force. (See further discussion of this concept in Part V of this book.) Once you make a basic decision that this is a person and a moment that invites the opportunity for a Me-You moment, the path is quite simple. Start with a smile. Then open your heart to whatever is meant to happen. Follow two very simple   principles, and success is moments away.

1. Ask, learn and use the person's name and give yours. Knowing and using the name immediately acknowledges this person, not just as a function, but, more importantly, as another human being.

2. Initiate some fresh, appropriate exchange beyond the scope of the task. Some genuine personal comment, ("What a lovely necklace!" "Great sweater. Where do you shop?") works well, or even the timeless standard, the weather. Come from a place of genuine interest and more times than not, your CP will meet you halfway.

If You Want More

Light listening is fine all of the time for some and some of the time for all. Light listeners tend to focus on what is spoken, and usually just the facts, or the external details of the topic. If that is enough, then stop here. No need to read more. But if you want deeper connections, conversations that contribute to growth and learning, then deep listening is what you're after. It is the bridge from acquaintanceship to friendship, and from friendship to understanding and intimacy. Deep Listening paves the way to share a sense of the sacred – however you may define it – with others, to cut through loneliness, to foster true caring and connection. Deep Listening is also the master tool that can transform us as a society, beyond the kind of divisive and polarized thought and talk that threatens us, back (and forward) to reclaim our traditional values and our democratic spirit (more on this in Step V).

We will explore Deep Listening in detail in the remaining chapters of Part 2 of this book.

Notes from the Journey

Core Awareness: Listening is a complex combination of attitudes and skills, that can be thought of as operating along a spectrum comprised of Non-Listening, Light listening, and Deep Listening.

Core Value: Curiosity, the desire to understand and support others.

Core Skill: Flexibility to speak and listen.

Core Tools: Light listening: An easy smile, an open heart, and a good question.

Next Steps

1. For your Conversational journal: Consider your listening strategy. When are you a non-listener? When a light listener? Are there certain people or circumstances that bring out one or another of these listening modes in you? Different topics? Different moods?

2. Deliberately, create at least one light listening conversation with a stranger or someone you know only slightly, every day for a week. Note in your journal what you did and how it worked. What's the cost? What's the benefit? Is it worth it?

Chapter 8
Dive Deeper

"I finally get what you mean by Deep Listening.
And it's so cool."

In my teen years, I was at a party, struggling to fit in as usual. I ate and drank too much and tried to blend into the walls, before settling my eyes on two girls, engaged in rapt conversation. I knew Jenny slightly. Something about her manner – the way she leaned toward the other girl, the steadiness of her eye contact, the way she nodded her head from time to time, how she'd occasionally reach out and touch the other girl on the arm – fascinated me. I was enchanted. And jealous. Whatever they were doing, I wanted to do too.

Years later I recognize the phenomenon of deep listening. I didn't have a name for it back then.

Mindful Listening – The Journey to Connection

Over the years, I grew in confidence and skill and came finally to value myself as a listener – less staring at my feet, less pretending to understand while totally lost, less awkward fumbling for direction, less anxiety, more satisfying, lasting friendships. I realized that deep listening is the foundation for good friendships. Not just for friendships, but for insights and learning new skills, for raising children, for intimacy, for solving problems at work, selling a project, relaxing at a party, even understanding and accepting myself. It's like pulling back the curtain and seeing the world in technicolor for the first time.

Deep Listening leads to deep understanding. Deep understanding is the basis for successful relationships. Disagreement based on ignorance of one another, by contrast, is the road to prejudice, resentment and strife. Deep listening, though too rarely taught, is a master life skill.

Deep Listening Defined[12]

Deep Listening is a way of receiving the full message – from yourself, from others, and from the world. Deep Listening, as I've indicated before, is the heart of Mindful Conversation.

You may be familiar with the concept of Active Listening.

Those who practice active listening have already moved far beyond Serial Monologue and grabbing response (Chapter 1). But Active Listening is a tool. Like a hammer, its impact depends on the hand that's swinging it. The tools of Mindful Conversation intimately tied together in a full person approach, apply body, mind and spirit to the universal human drive to connect and express.

Deep Listening is:

o Temporarily setting aside your own judgments, stories and opinions

o So that you can gift your CP with undivided attention

o In order to grasp the full meaning of both spoken and unspoken messages

o And thereby connect deeply.

Deep listening builds on the skills of active listening, but goes far beyond active listening. It includes the overall values and principles of Mindful Conversation. Beyond any concept of mere silent attending, it includes appropriate questioning and feedback; it filters out distracted thought and action; it includes listening beneath the spoken words, reaching for submerged thought, feelings and meaning. It becomes the basis for a different kind of relationship, a shift of both mind and heart.

Two Dialogues

Our friend Martha, is back, this time with her friend Lisa. Martha and Lisa meet for a drink after work. Here are two versions, numbered for reference later, of their dialogue.

Dialogue A:

1. Lisa: So, Martha, how is that teen-age daughter of yours these days?

2. Martha: Abby. She's okay, I guess.

3. Lisa: That's good. Is she still with that same boyfriend?

4. Martha: Yeah. She doesn't tell me much about him.

5. Lisa: Do you see him much?

6. Martha: No, I've told her he's not welcome at the house. (She pauses.) Most of last week my own daughter wouldn't even talk to me.

7. Lisa: You banned him from the house?

8. Martha: I don't want him around. But she sneaks out at night and meets him.

9. Lisa: Sneaks out after she's gone to bed?

10. Martha: He's no good for her. I'm so worried.

11. Lisa: Teenagers, they're impossible! I went through the same kind of thing with my daughter Crystal. Hopeless.

12. Martha: What's going to happen to her?

13. Lisa: Don't worry. She'll grow out of it. It just takes time. Crystal thought I was the devil in disguise. Now she's happily married and has a job. Imagine!

Lisa is a good friend. She likes Martha and wants to support her. She is, in fact, a good active listener. She inquires (1, 3, 5) She echoes what she's heard (7), and checks for understanding (9). She summarizes the dilemma (11). She gives encouragement (13). So, what's missing?

Martha will leave this conversation perhaps having experienced some reprieve, but still burdened by the problem and her feelings about herself and her daughter. She may appreciate Lisa's trying to help, but she is unlikely to feel understood or acknowledged. She may even feel more alone and hopeless in her relationship with Abby.

Let's replay the Martha / Lisa dialogue now that Lisa has embraced Deep Listening:

Dialogue B:

1. Lisa: So, Martha, how is that teen-age daughter of yours behaving these days?

2. Martha: Abby. She's okay, I guess.

3. Lisa: Just okay? What does that mean?

4. Martha: I've been studying Parent Effectiveness. It's okay, I guess. I don't know. I think she doesn't want to talk to me anymore.

5. Lisa: "Doesn't talk much." How so? Sounds like you're pretty cut off.

6. Martha: Mmm. It's the boyfriend, Rodney. I told her he's not welcome in my house. Drugs and insults. He mistreats her, no good for her. It's a huge source of conflict between us. Most of last week she wouldn't even speak to me.

7. Lisa: Oh, Martha, that must be so hard.

8. Martha: I'm worried sick about her.

9. Lisa: You really love Abby, don't you?

10. Martha: (Showing the first sign of a smile) Oh, yes. Yes, I love her so much, and I feel so incapable to help her. I can't even talk with her. I feel like such a failure.

11. Lisa: Parenting is so hard. (She reaches over to touch Martha's hand.) You're going through a really rough time, but that doesn't make you a failure. We all go through hard times. I sure have with Crystal.

12. Martha: She's slipping away. I've tried everything I know. I don't know what's going to happen to her. (She looks away.)

13. Lisa: (After a period of silence) Martha, I believe in you. I see how you care. You know I've often questioned my own

readiness to be a mother. There are times I think I'm not cut out for it.

14. Martha: You, really? You always seem like the perfect mom.

15. Lisa: Hardly. I lose it frequently. We all do.

16. Martha: You don't think I'm hopeless?

17. Lisa: Abby is so fortunate to have you as her mom ... even if she won't talk to you right now.

How different this conversation is from Dialogue A, which was already a far more connected conversation than the typical Serial Monologue with its signature grabbing response.

Curiosity helps Lisa take Martha down through the three distinct layers of personal exploration (first introduced in the Pyramid of Connection, Chapter 2):

1. Facts. She has a teenage daughter. She's studying Parent Effectiveness.

2. Thoughts / Feelings. "She doesn't want to talk to me anymore."

3. Thoughts / Feelings. "You really love Abby, don't you?"

4. Personal Meaning. "You're going through a really rough time, but that doesn't make you a failure."

Rather than simply parroting the facts, she invites Martha to share how she's feeling (3, 5, 7). She taps into the unspoken theme (9), giving hope and perspective to Martha's dark point of view. Lisa hears the underlying story that Martha is telling herself and gently, but firmly confronts her (11). This is the personal meaning, how the speaker sees herself, the story she tells herself. In this case, Martha views herself as a failure. Lisa uses appropriate non-verbal support (11). She briefly shares her own, parallel struggle (11, 13, 15). Without rushing in to give advice or to solve Martha's problem, she provides comfort and support, and gives Martha what she most needs, a sense of hope (15).

Lisa's listening is light years beyond the average active listener. When you listen deeply, you are not just passively listening. You are actually inviting others to explore their deeper themes with you. You are demonstrating the values of the C.A.R.E. model.

THE C.A.R.E. MODEL IN ACTION

To more fully appreciate what Lisa does, let's return to the C.A.R.E. model (Introduced in Chapter 2).

- o **C** - Curiosity
- o **A** - Authenticity
- o **R** - Respect
- o **E** - Empathy

Curiosity

Lisa's intention is not just to look good, impress or give advice. Or to tell her own story. Her whole being is focused on opening the door of acceptance, connection and exploration.

Curiosity is the pathway to discovery, for both listener and speaker. Notice how Lisa uses a combination of inquiry and echoing to draw Martha out, to gently help her to clarify what she means beyond generalizations such as "She's okay" and "We don't talk much." She listens under the words to the unspoken message, "Sounds like you're missing her." Martha didn't say that, but Lisa infers it, and floats it as a trial balloon.

We express curiosity in many ways: open body language, eye contact, paraphrasing what you hear, asking appropriate questions, acknowledging stated opinions (even if you disagree), inquiring about unexpressed thoughts or feelings.

The common enemies of curiosity are judgment, fear of sounding naive or stupid, making assumptions and closed mindedness.

Curiosity doesn't mean agreement with another's point of view. We may not even fully understand it. We do need to be curious.

Authenticity

Authentic conversation is about listening and speaking in a real and open way. It requires allowing yourself to feel and to express the full range of thought and emotion, whether it's light and joyous or awkward and inconvenient.

Being authentic means discarding the mask, being willing to appear silly, confused, or unreasonable; open to feeling and expressing sadness, anger, even hopelessness. In short, daring to be vulnerable. Notice how Lisa shares (without "grabbing" the conversation) her own fears and insecurities. "You know I've often questioned my own readiness to be a mother. There are times I think I'm not cut out for it."

We all develop masks, to hide from pain and embarrassment.

Yet it is the removing of these masks and daring to be vulnerable, that makes us truly strong and fully human. When we set our masks aside, others trust us and are drawn in by our authenticity. They are likely to open up in response. This is the pathway to true connection. Connection is the first step towards intimacy.

Brené Brown has written especially eloquently about the role of vulnerability in life. In *Daring Greatly,* she writes, "Vulnerability is not knowing victory or defeat, it's understanding the necessity of both; its engaging. It's being all in." Authenticity requires us to set aside the games we play in favor of being "all in."

Recently, I was talking with an old friend. She's brilliant at her work. She was talking about her work challenges when suddenly she stopped, mid-sentence, as if she'd felt a rumble in the earth. I waited, not knowing. Silence engulfed us. She dropped her gaze. When she began again, her voice was laced in melancholy. "Last Sunday, when I, for once, wasn't working, I came to a standstill. I didn't know what to do with myself. I no longer know who I am beyond work. This is not who I want to be."

The vulnerability of her remark drew me to her. I've been there too. We were one in our common journey. When the mask drops, the connection is deep, lasting and satisfying. This is authentic conversation.

My friend led the way, removing the mask of competence and feigned control to reveal her more vulnerable side. She "dared greatly" and won the day. I modeled deep listening – by remaining present, attentive and silent. Silence is hard work. Easier to cover up ("Don't worry. We all feel that way sometimes.") or change the topic. Once we had crossed the threshold, there was no turning back. Truth seeks the light. It is our defenses that keep us locked in darkness.

People who speak authentically and show their vulnerabilities win trust. Try it. You'll discover that more people actually want to talk with you, listen deeper to you, share their own deeper being with you. This is connection.

Respect

We all want respect – for our ideas, our efforts, our feelings, who we are. Deep Listening is respect made audible. But many people never experience the sense of acknowledgment that comes from being listened to in this way. When I am listened to respectfully, my heart opens and my truth tumbles out. The talk may be trying or painful. But if I feel respected, I leave the conversation feeling whole again.

The obstacles to respectful listening lurk everywhere: interruption, distraction, impatience, judgment, disinterest, narcissism ... on and on. Poor listening habits are deep, and habits are hard to change. The goal is not perfection, but to keep the value of respect in the forefront of even the most difficult conversation.

Even if we disagree, we can disagree respectfully. Focus on the behavior, the action, or the idea, rather than the person.

Avoid name calling. Never, "You're lazy." Rather, "It seems to me that you don't follow through."

Empathy

Empathy is the ability to understand and be sensitive to the feelings of another. Very different from sympathy, which means feeling pity or sorrow for another's misfortune. And never argue with someone else's feelings. Feelings are not right or wrong; they just are.

Empathy is the pathway into another's world and perhaps the most far-reaching skill of Deep Listening. If you practice empathy regularly, you will, over time, develop curiosity, authenticity and respect. "Ultimately, the greatest service you can provide for another is your full attention," writes blogger Carol Putnam (*www.carolputnam.com*).

Your full, empathic attention is what we're talking about here - thoughts, feelings and actions. Empathy is not passive. To be empathic means being able to recognize what others are expressing, whether verbally or non-verbally. This requires thought. It also involves being able to "get it" emotionally. This requires feeling. And it involves the willingness to support another person in their pain or suffering. This requires action.

Bringing it All Together

Deep Listening is an expression of caring – for yourself, and your CP and for the promise of connection. It is a behavior, but more deeply, a way of being.

Be clear in your intentions. Deep Listening can flow only from an intention to connect, to understand and to express.

There is no memorized game plan, no script and no rule book. In difficult conversations, technique-based approaches such as active listening tend to be blown aside by the emotion, stress and pressure. Mindful Conversation is subject to all the same forces, but the foundation of values and intention gives it staying power far beyond any technique.

Listen before speaking. Mindful Conversation rests on the belief that it is generally most effective to listen first and then speak. For many, the unconscious goal is to speak first, longest, and loudest. On the other hand, if your intention is to connect and understand, then by definition, you will conduct yourself differently.

Pay attention to what is said, and to what is not said. Whether from shyness, confusion, or misplaced humility, many people hesitate to speak their deepest truths. That, of course, is everyone's right. But listen beneath the spoken words, for the unspoken feelings, the untold story, the self-limiting beliefs, the distorted thinking. These are the key to deep, authentic connection. Words can be expressive, but they can also mask and distort. Listen with the ears of your heart.

A Word of Caution

In the next chapter, we will dive into the specific tools that you can use to implement the intentions discussed above. These tools are the "science," the observable, measurable behaviors that mark Reflective Listening. But first, a word of caution.

Reflective Listening is not a panacea. It does not guarantee harmony and deep connection in every conversation, and, like any process, it can be manipulated. Deep Listening can be misused, either as a way to avoid authentic and open dialogue, or as a way to manipulate or control others. You can listen to someone to ingratiate yourself, or to trick them into trusting you and revealing information that you can then use against them. This is not Mindful Conversation.

The choice of when and with whom to go deep is yours. Use it authentically and respectfully. Use it to deepen the fullness of life, yours and your CP's.

Notes from the Journey

Core Awareness: Deep listening is the heart of Mindful Conversation.

Core Value: Empathy. Deep Listen with the ears of the heart.

Core Skill: Setting aside the mask and the ego, to attend fully to another.

Core Tools: Reflection, Inquiry.

Next Steps

1. Think of someone whom you consider to be a really good listener. Write about him/ her. What specific, observable behaviors tell you that she is listening? What is it like to be listened to in this way? Consider telling this person about the quality of their listening and what it does for you.

2. What gets in the way of your listening? Are you hampered by not understanding the importance? By lacking the skill? By being overtaken by emotions that block your intent to listen? Think about a recent time when you were not the kind of listener you'd like to be. Look inside yourself to analyze what got in your way.

3. If you develop the skills and habit of deep listening, what difference might it make in your life? Your relationships?

4. Make a date to talk with someone you trust, about deep listening. If you like, set up a ground rule that for half the time you will talk, and he will listen. For the second half, he talks, and you listen. Give each other feedback on the quality of your listening.

Chapter 9
Your Tool Box: Verbal Tools

"Heavy? No. These are my tools for listening.
I never go anywhere without them."

If you want to build a home, you need many tools and you need to know how to use each of them. Conversation is a kind of home. Find the tools that work best for you. Adapt them to your particular situation, the conversations and relationships that you have or want to nurture. Then build your dream home.

Practice is the path. Discover which tools work best for you. Use them in different combinations. Make them your own.

Verbal Tools

This chapter is the most common, very practical verbal tools to enhance your listening. Each tool is defined, with an example, benefits of use, best practices, and most common mistakes.

1. Echo

2. Summarize

3. Perception Check

4. Closed-ended Questions

5. Open-ended Questions

6. Attending Phrases

7. Clarifying Conversational Ground Rules

8. Attending to non-verbal messages

9. Managing tone, pitch, and volume

1. ECHO ⏵⏵)

Definition:
Repeating back the essential words as spoken by your CP.

Example:
Speaker: I have two assignments due tomorrow, and I have to work all day today. I don't see how I can even show up in class.

Listener: You have assignments due tomorrow and a full workday today. You can't imagine going to class.

Benefits:
This tool communicates to the speaker that you have listened and taken in their message. It's like a mirror, enabling the speaker to "see" herself. Used appropriately, it encourages the

speaker to continue and further develop the topic.

Being heard is an enormously affirming event. A simple "echo" of what someone says can give your CP a sense of being understood, of not being alone in whatever situation they're dealing with.

Many people have never experienced being truly heard! If you do nothing more than echo another's words, you demonstrate respect, caring, and understanding. In effect, you communicate that your CP is worthy of your time and attention. If you've never tried this, give it a shot. Then see if you can assess the impact.

Best Practices:

Use the echo to confirm that you've heard what's been said, whenever you are not sure if you have heard correctly, or periodically to confirm your connection and attention to the speaker.

Repeat not just the words, but echo the tone and volume of the speaker. Mirror the speaker's body language.

Use mostly the speaker's actual phrasing and word choice.

Common Mistakes:

The echo can be overused or used in a mechanical, monotone way that undermines its benefits. Be mindful of your basic intention, to understand and connect. This is person-to-person, not robot-to-person conversation. Reflect the speaker's tone (excited, sad, apprehensive, etc.) as well as the words.

Avoid adding your own interpretations or rephrasing, and especially advice giving. This is not the time.

2. SUMMARIZE (AKA PARAPHRASING) 📋

Definition:

Summarizing or restating the speaker's message in your own language; checking for confirmation.

Example:

Speaker: Gives rambling account of his day.

Listener: "Sounds like you had a really rough day – car troubles, multiple frustrations at work, a lunch date that evaporated. Am I hearing you correctly?"

Benefits:

Helps a speaker to hear the essence of what he's saying. Can cut out irrelevant or disjointed material. Helps to focus a conversation.

Summarizing is particularly useful if the conversation has wandered or you suspect your CP may have lost sight of the main thread. Or if you've become confused. Or to take stock of what's going on.

Best Practices:

When paraphrasing, don't be afraid to use your own language, but be sure to confirm your understanding, i.e., "Sounds to me like your chief concern is about not having a backup plan in case of rain. Is that what you're worried about?"

Don't worry if you haven't understood everything. Even if you get it wrong, it can be helpful to a speaker to clarify again what they are trying to communicate. Rarely will someone take offense, if they see that you are trying to understand.

In your own talk, reflect the mood, as well as the facts, of the speaker's message.

Keep your summary short. This is about the speaker, not about you.

Common Mistakes:

Don't fake it. If you are lost, admit it. "I'm sorry, but I've really lost track of your main concern. What would you say is the main problem?"

3. PERCEPTION CHECK ♡

Definition:
Suggest an underlying or implied thought, feeling or personal meaning, that you infer from what the speaker has said. The Perception Check goes beyond the echo or summary, to suggest an interpretation of what the speaker is communicating.

Example:
Speaker: "I just came back from the dentist, who tells me I need a root canal. Milly was home from school all day, and my husband is away on business. That might make life easier, except that the garage door won't open, and my car was due in the shop. What do I do?"

Listener: "Wow. Sounds like you're understandably overwhelmed by all you have to deal with. You're looking for some help in how to handle all of this. Is that it?"

Benefits:
The listener now gets the benefit of your subjective interpretation of her communication. She is free to accept or disagree with how you see it.

Best Practices:
Perception Check is a trial balloon. Use language that suggests you understand, but isn't arrogant or insistent. Try, "Sounds like ..." or "I hear you saying ..." or "You seem to be saying ..." or "Is it ..."

If your CP doesn't pick up on your interpretation, it's usually best to back off. If you're with someone whom you know to be open about their inner world, then you are probably o.k. Tread lightly if the speaker has not made any reference to feelings or personal meaning.

As ever, mirror you CP's tone and body language as much as practical.

Common Mistakes:

Some people are more open, while others are protective and sensitive about their inner world. Stay tuned in to how your words are being received. It's very easy (and unhelpful) to take over, i.e., "grab" the conversation, and give unsolicited advice.

Timing is everything. Listen deeply and watch your CP's facial and body language for clues. Do not rush in too early. The body gives clues that are often more reliable than words. (See Chapter 12 for more on this.)

Language like "I know just how you feel" is presumptuous and off-putting. You don't know how they feel. That's why you need to listen.

Avoid telling your own story, or lathering on the sympathy.

4. CLOSED ENDED QUESTIONS

Definition:

Questions that have a clearly right or wrong answer, can be answered by "Yes" or "No," or have a very limited pool of possible answers, such as a number, a fact, a location, a time, etc. Multiple choice and True/False questions are examples of closed ended questions. "Did you eat breakfast this morning?" Closed ended questions often begin with Who? What? Where? When? How many?

Example:

Listener: "Let me be sure I understood. You were there at 5 p.m., but no one else showed up until 6. Is that right?"

Benefits:

Closed ended questions are particularly useful when you're trying to get at the facts of a situation. They are short and focused, and thus relatively quick to ask and respond to.

Best Practices:

Use to clarify or gather facts, or when you are genuinely interrogating someone.

Explain why you are probing. "I want to make sure I've understood what happened."

Intersperse closed ended questions with other tools, such as echo or summarizing or open ended questions.

Common Mistakes:

Overuse of closed ended questions or an aggressive, demanding tone makes you sound like a prosecutor and often brings on defensiveness in your CP. Avoid asking a lot of closed ended questions all in a row.

Generally, avoid closed ended questions when you are getting to know someone, primarily motivated by a desire to connect, trying to understand deeper motivations, thoughts or feelings.

5. OPEN ENDED QUESTIONS

Definition:

Questions that have no right or wrong answer and cannot be answered with a simple "yes" or "no." Such questions often start with "why?" "how?" or "what?" The answers are frequently subjective.

Example:

Speaker: "So, I told him I'd think it over, and he just walked away. I haven't heard from him since then."

Listener: "Can you imagine or even guess what might have been going on for him?"

Benefits:

Non-judgmental, open ended questions demonstrate respect, a desire to understand, and curiosity. They are a window into another's experience or a topic of interest, a doorway to learning.

Best Practices:

To take a conversation deeper, focus on "why" and "how" questions. Avoid any tone of judgment or inquisition. Ask one question at a time. Keep it simple. Revert to echo, summarize, and perception check frequently.

Be mindful of your intention, to understand. Wrap your questions in respect and empathy.

Ask your question and then pause. Listen carefully and give time for a response. Don't rush in to fill the silence if there is some.

Common Mistakes:

Many people never or rarely ask a question of any kind! The worst mistake is not to ask. But too many questions can overwhelm the speaker. Think before asking, then choose your words carefully.

6. BRIEF ATTENDING PHRASES 👍

Definition:
Verbal clues that confirm listening and understanding.
Example:
"I see." "Oh, yes." "Uh huh." "I understand." "Okay." "Sure." "Wow!" "Really." Etc.

Benefits:
Gives frequent reassurance and support that you are engaged and listening. Encourages continued dialogue and discovery.

Best Practices:
Use, but don't overuse. Combine with appropriate non- verbal cues such as eye contact and head nods.

Vary the phrase. Speak, even these short phrases, with conviction and sincerity.

Match the speaker's tone and body language where practical. If the speaker is subdued, respond in a somewhat equal tone. This tool is not about cheerleading. It's about drawing another person out, understanding. If the speaker is excited, it's great to match their enthusiasm for the moment.

Common Mistakes:

Like the echo, this tool can degenerate into a rote, mechanical sounding response. Stay alert to what your CP is really trying to communicate. Be alert to shifts in mood and tone. Speak authentically, never by rote.

7. ESTABLISH / CONFIRM PROCESS GROUND RULES ⚙

Definition:

Ask for or suggest guidance on how best to proceed. Clarify process issues such as time availability, topics, ground rules, goals, roles, location, mood, etc.

Example:

"Just to let you know, I have twenty minutes available, then I have to leave. Will that work?"

"Are you looking for advice? Or should I just listen?"

"Let's take some time to define the problem first, before we talk about solutions."

"Here are three things I'd like to talk about. What about you?

Do you have specific topics you want to discuss?"

"I know this is a sensitive subject. I want to be helpful. Please let me know if I'm probing too much or getting in the way."

Benefits:

An effective conversation depends on "process agreements" (how we're going to talk) as well as content agreements (what we're going to talk about). Take a moment, often at the start, to set the conversation up for success, by establishing the process. Establishing ground rules can help prevent communication problems before they happen. If the conversation breaks down in the middle, it's never too late to step back and re-confirm or discuss process agreements that you need to have in place, for example, "It seems like we're both interrupting each other. How about if we slow down and agree not to interrupt?"

Best Practices:

This tool may be most useful in formal settings such as groups and meetings, but can also be useful in social settings. Although it may be counter-cultural, don't be shy to suggest process agreements that you think will help the conversation.

Common Mistakes:

Sensing that something is off, but never raising the issue, thereby missing the opportunity to self-correct.

8. PAY ATTENTION TO NON-VERBAL 🏆 MESSAGES

Definition:

Being conscious of and inquiring, as appropriate, about non-verbal messages.

Example:

"When you began talking about that time, your whole demeanor changed. You smiled, sat up straight, even your voice smiled. Why do you think that might be?"

"When you mentioned Evra, you slumped in your chair and looked at the floor. Your whole facial expression dropped. You seemed like a different person."

Benefits:
Don't be fooled by words alone. Non-verbal messages are often the best clue to what your CP is really thinking or feeling.

Best Practices:
Keep your eyes and your intuition open to non-verbal messages. Check for congruence between verbal and non- verbal messages. Consider naming, but not judging, what you see, e.g., "You appeared to be excited about this topic at the beginning, but now you sound withdrawn. Has something shifted?"

Understand that if there is a discrepancy between verbal and non-verbal messages, the non-verbal message often is the more reliable.

Appropriate response may vary greatly depending on circumstance and relationship. Always be sensitive to power dynamics, timing, outside influences, mood, etc.

Common Mistakes:
Failure to notice or inquire as appropriate when a CP's non-verbal messages seem incongruent or confusing. For example, if your CP shifts mood, goes silent, seems distracted or withdrawn, don't ignore such signs. As a minimum, notice. If appropriate, name the behavior. If it seems like a detriment to effective conversation, surface the issue for possible exploration.

9. MANAGE YOUR OWN TONE, 📢 PITCH, AND VOLUME.

Definition:

Ensuring congruence between *what* you say, and *how* you say it.

"Negative" Example:

"Oh, that's so sweet of you." (Spoken with dripping sarcasm.)
"I'd love to have dinner with you." (Spoken with flat affect.)

Benefits:

Your CP's (like you) will pay more attention to your affect than your words. To be a powerful communicator, be sure that your words and your non-verbal affect are in sync.

Best Practices:

Be intentional about the effect of your messaging.

Communication is effective when the words, the music and the dance all say the same thing.

Be aware of tone, the quality of your voice. Is it gentle or harsh; compassionate or judging? Enthusiastic or bored?

Be aware of pitch: High, shrill or modulated? Be aware of volume: Soft or loud?

Be aware of pacing: Calm or frenzied?

Be aware of body posture: Engaged or withdrawn?

Common Mistakes:

Being unaware of body language or sending an incongruent message, expecting that the words will be believed regardless of how they are spoken. Incongruence between the words and the tone, pitch or volume creates confusion at best; mistrust at worst.

Notes from the Journey

Core Awareness: Mindful Conversation requires a full toolbox of verbal and non-verbal tools

Core Value: These tools support all four primary values of the C.A.R.E. Model: Curiosity, Awareness, Respect and Empathy.

Core Skill: Consciously combining the various tools, "listening" for both verbal and non-verbal feedback

Core Tools: All of them. Find your favorites. Use frequently and with pride.

Next Steps

1. Learn and use the name. This requires focus. Set yourself a goal, for example, if you're at a party, to ask and learn 3 new names. You can practice in stores, at church, in a class, bar or wherever. Listen when you first ask, then use the name immediately after you learn it. "Great to meet you, Paula." Think about the name as you say it. Commit to use the name at least twice, once at the beginning and once at the end of the conversation. "I enjoyed talking with you, Paula."

2. When first meeting someone, do a quick scan for some item that awakens your curiosity and inquire about it. Use the item to open a deeper conversation. Possibilities are limitless. For example, "What an unusual ring. I bet there's a story behind that?" Who knows where a simple remark like that might lead? If you're open.

Chapter 10
Use the Tools: Non-verbal

"You don't say much, Fred, but your non-verbal language says it's all over. Is that what you're saying?"

He was a large man in every way. He towered over me, his shoulders big enough to seem he was wearing shoulder pads. His extra weight and back troubles made it hard for him to bend low, but he compensated by moving around his organization with the confidence of power. I had worked with Henry (not his real name) a year earlier, helping him resolve some tricky relationships.

When I was rehired for some further work with his organization, I went gladly. Henry was there. He strode over and put his big hand on my shoulder. "Good to see you, again.

Of course, I remember the work you did with us, how much it helped. One thing in particular."

I try to keep my ego under control, but it's always nice to hear compliments. "I remember ..." He paused. I waited, wondering what it was that I had said that had had such an impact.

"We were seated around a table," he continued. "I had dropped my pen on the floor, and was struggling to get down to pick it up. You came over, picked it up for me, and walked away. I doubt that anyone else even noticed. I'm embarrassed about my size, as you know. I'll never forget that wordless gesture."

Conversation happens on many levels. Non-verbal messages often make the most lasting impact.

The Power of Non-Verbal Language

Without language, our brains could never have guided us to our position at the top of the food chain. Words allow us to investigate and discover, to analyze and describe, to create, to reason, to problem solve, to remember, and to plan ... but also to distort and to obfuscate. The language of most human brains is predominantly verbal, but the language of the heart is more often non-verbal.

Joy is communicated instantly through the smile, and usually only later, with words. Sadness is immediately recognizable, whether words confirm or mask it. Anger, hope, stress, surprise, fear, disgust, approval – for all such emotions, the non-verbal signals are the prevailing currency across culture, time and language. You can and do, whether consciously or not, say a lot without ever uttering a word. Posture, tone, facial expression, physical gesture, eye contact – each of these serves either to reinforce or to contradict your verbal message. Many experts say that non-verbal signals account for at least 60% of what gets received and remembered. Does the per cent really matter? [13]

Have you ever talked with someone who makes no eye contact, or who is clearly looking around the room, who yawns, fidgets or taps away at their cell phone as you talk? This is "non-listening" in the extreme. As a listener, if you take in only the words, you will likely miss the message.

Check out this brief dialogue between two friends:

Roger: Sam, good to see you. How's it going?

Sam:(Looking down) Fine. And you?

Roger: Great. Last time we talked, I remember you were struggling at work. Things better now?

Sam:(Barely audible) It's o.k.

Roger: Time takes care of all things, eh?

Sam:(Nods. Fidgets.)

Roger: I knew you'd work it out.

Roger has done a decent job of active listening, reflecting Sam's verbal message, but he has totally misunderstood Sam. Words can be consciously or unconsciously manipulated. In this case, Sam (perhaps) is feeling embarrassed or ashamed. Or maybe he is distracted by something else. We don't know what's really going on. His words say that things are fine, but his non-verbal message telegraphs the opposite. If you were Roger, which would you believe?

In being "deaf" to Sam's non-verbal message, Roger has badly misunderstood his friend.

If Roger were really listening, he would notice Sam's demeanor and reflect that back, demonstrating interest and empathy. Had he "heard" Sam's "hidden" message, their dialogue would have been very different, hopefully more in accord with the C.A.R.E. Model. Non-verbal language is present in every conversation, whether noticed or not, and often, it is the most reliable messenger.

I am frequently reminded of the vital role of non-verbal messaging, when my wife, Wendy, and I get into a difficult conversation. We try with words to sort things out. Sometimes this works, but sometimes not. And then one or the other of us will smile, or make genuine eye contact, or reach out and touch, or offer a hug. The non-verbal message often improves things instantly, whereas a long, protracted conversation had not. These are magical moments. Words are great but limited. Non-verbal language can show in a second what words sometimes are unable to say in an hour. When you want to repair or connect, when words don't cut it, smile or touch (appropriately). Use the right tool for the job.

Types of Nonverbal Expression

Beyond voice, there are four principle avenues for non-verbal expression: [14]

1. Appearance

2. Facial Expression

3. Body Language / Gesture

4. Touch

1. APPEARANCE 👁

The first impression that sighted people receive from our CP's has nothing to do with words. It is visual. In the first seconds of a conversation, most of us form some kind of judgment based mostly on visual cues. This assessment may turn out to be completely inaccurate, but because it is first, it is often lasting.

Think for a moment about the key features that you (often unconsciously) take in when you meet a stranger. Typical are age, gender, race, culture of origin, facial expression, body shape and size, attractiveness, energy level. In the first 10 seconds, we make assumptions such as: this person is like me (or not), healthy (or not), friendly (or not), local (or not), prosperous (or not), trustworthy (or not), interesting (or not). Before saying a word, you make judgments, positive or negative. Likewise, they are forming opinions of you. Who needs words?

2. FACIAL EXPRESSION ☺☺

We all, always, have a facial expression, even if it is blank.

Your facial expression imparts a quick but often lasting impression. Cosmetic companies wish us to believe otherwise, but we have minimal control over the physical features and dimensions of our face. But emotion is another matter. Despite vast differences in social expression and norms across the globe, facial expression of the basic human emotions appears to be quite similar across most cultures. The six <u>basic</u> human emotions (happiness, sadness, fear, anger, surprise and disgust) are relatively easy to interpret. If you pay attention.

A skillful reflective listener pays equal attention to the face, and especially the eyes, as to the words spoken. Make it a habit to study the eyes of your CP's. See if you can "read" the eyes.

3. BODY LANGUAGE 🏃

Body language is a constant communicator. How aware are you of your body language? Of other people's?

We easily recognize an aggressive posture, but the body also telegraphs peace, or boredom, impatience, or anxiety. Posture can connote confidence and determination or fear and resignation. It's not always easy to interpret body language. Be observant but cautious. Don't judge too quickly. A jittery leg or foot may indicate nervousness, but it is also a common habit.

Folded arms are often described as a posture of resistance or anger, but can also indicate that your CP is cold.

When in doubt, check it out. Ask: "You lowered your eyes and frowned when you talked about Jack. How are you feeling about him now?"

How you sit or stand sends a message, whether intentional or not. Especially when sitting, leaning slightly forward generally communicates interest. Slouching or folding the arms may communicate disinterest or closed mindedness. When you are in listening mode, a good strategy is to mirror the body language of the speaker. If your CP leans in, follow suit.

Likewise if she leans back. This copycat movement can signal to someone that you are listening under the words, to the tone of what they're saying or feeling.

Heads and hands can communicate a world in a single gesture. A shoulder shrug generally indicates that you don't care. A tiny shake of the head or eyes rolling back says, "No." Similarly, a slight nod, especially if accompanied by a smile, says , "Yes."

Some people like and effectively use hand gestures to communicate a lot. Others hate them. Open palms can communicate an open, accepting attitude. A fist may communicate tension or aggression. Almost any part of the body can be used to communicate. Think of the power of a thumbs up (or down) or high five. Many gestures communicate very different meanings in different cultures, so it's important to be culturally aware.

4. APPROPRIATE TOUCH

Touch is a powerful conversation tool when used sensitively, dangerous and potentially very harmful when used unconsciously or inappropriately. A touch can be casual or intimate. The possibilities range from a handshake or small touch on the arm, to a pat on the back, hugging, kissing, holding hands or taking someone's arm while walking. Cultural and individual attitudes and interpretations of any single touch vary widely. An occasional touch on the arm can signal a delightful level of trust and connection, or send totally the wrong signal. The best guidance is to proceed slowly, and with caution, especially if there is any chance of misinterpretation. Stay aware of the feedback you are getting. Is your touch welcomed and understood? Or is there resistance and/or confusion?

Some people do not like to be touched, even lightly. Some gestures, such as touching your own heart, can simulate a sense of empathy for another, without ever actually touching the other person.

Physical Space

How close or far away you stand (or sit) sends a message. What is "crowding" for one person may feel like "close and cozy" to another. Be aware and sensitive to others. Be responsive to feedback you get, often non-verbal. Experiment and see what responses you get.

Silence

Or the "sacred pause" **is the quintessential nonverbal tool, one that is** too rarely used as a conscious conversational aid. Many people are so fearful of silence that they rush in to fill even the briefest moment of silence with chatter, anything to fill the void. But managed appropriately, silence is a powerful tool. Allow silence and wait. You might be surprised at what shows up. (See Ch 11 for more on this topic.)

Notes from the Journey

Core Awareness: Non-verbal communication often accounts for around 60 of the message that is received. There are four main avenues of non-verbal expression: appearance, facial expression, body language and touch.

Core Value: Awareness. Non-verbal messages are often processed unconsciously. Turn up the awareness meter.

Core Skill: Noticing and attending to the nonverbal communication, but deferring judgment.

Core Tools: Eyes. Don't just listen. Watch!

Next Steps

1. Turn off your hearing. Tune in to other sensory inputs. If you are listening to a conversation, but not particularly involved, experiment with "turning off" the sound. See how much you can perceive just by watching the non-verbal signals.

2. Next time you are in a conversation with significant emotional content, focus on your CP's non-verbal communication. What particular forms of expression do you see? After the conversation, write down as many non-verbal indicators as you can remember, and what "message" you think each conveyed.

Chapter 11
The Pause that Refreshes

A: *"I told a joke. You could laugh."*

   Z: *"It wasn't funny."*

   A: *"It wasn't meant to be funny."*

   Z: *"Then it's not a joke. A joke is meant to be funny."*

   A: *"Yes, that's the funny part."*

   Z: *"You're not funny."*

   A: *"I'm not a joke."*

   Z: *"You are a joke."*

   A: *"Am I funny?"*

   Z: *"No, you're not funny."*

   A: *"You said I was a joke. A joke is funny, you said so."*

   Z: *"Well, you're not funny."*

   A: *"So I am a joke, but I'm not funny."*

   Z: *"You are not funny."*

   A: *"That's the funny part. You missed the joke. "*

In the midst of serious conversation, we must never forget the "pause that refreshes" (to borrow from the famous Coca-Cola ad).

This "Pause," a break from seriousness, manifests in several guises. I'll dub them "play, humor, and silence." Each of these represents a kind of pause in the action, a release of tension, a recognition that there is always light, even in dark times, if we will just slow down and allow.

Play

How do you play in conversation? Each of us has our own preferences. Sometimes the playful muse takes over. The circumstance, the topic, or the person you're with, or the chemistry between all of these, lights up the playful side of you. If you feel the urge to play, I encourage you to indulge it. Let go, let it happen, let joy flow freely.

The primary principle in the pause that refreshes is to expect joy, discover its hiding places, entertain it, encourage it in whatever ways make sense to you. When you believe joy can happen, you open the door. And in walks joy. Perhaps it's ridiculous to talk about how to *deliberately* bring out the *spontaneous* sense of joy and play within. So, let's be ridiculous. Here are 5 absurd ways to promote spontaneous fun in your conversation.

1. Before a particular conversation, set an intention to play, to have fun, to indulge your joy bone. Let that intention guide you to delicious places. Put joy and good fellowship into your voice, your smile, your words and your gestures. Look directly in someone else's eyes with joy in yours. You may be surprised. Or not.

2. Imagine your sense of joy and play as a fountain, that shoots delicious water high above you, regularly. Just because. Imagine yourself as that fountain.

Turn on the water. Let it loose. Let it splish and splash. If you don't like fountains, pick whatever object represents flowing joy to you. Visualize yourself as a spinning top, a singing bird, or your favorite sit com. Whatever stands for joy in your mind.

3. Laugh at yourself. Laughing at others is no-good, but laughing at yourself is fun and good therapy. Think of the silliest thing you've done in the past few days. Develop it into a story (See Chapter 15). Tell it. Laugh. Invite others to laugh with you.

4. Do you have a relationship with a Goddess of Fun? If not, try it now. Give her a name, a shape, an image. Learn from the ancient Greeks. Get to know the Goddess of Fun. Euphrosyne was the Greek goddess of Good Cheer, Joy and Mirth. Would you like to have her at your side? You can. Draw her, create a collage, write about her, or express the spirit of fun in any way you wish. Show your handiwork to a friend. Or don't show it to a friend. Now take it with you, inside your heart or inside your purse.

5. Ignore all of the above. Just know that you have a delightful, fun, playful side of you that can be there for you when you want it. Do you want it?

Start by talking about what you enjoy. Don't keep it a secret. Whatever it is, share it. Describe it. Find people who have a similar interest. Explore and revel in whatever it is that floats your boat. Gather and tell stories about it. Explain why you enjoy it so much. Let your voice sing and let your heart soar. Passion is infectious.

Beyond particular topics, there are so many approaches to

experiment with. Even if you are reticent by nature, invite the performer (See Chapter 4) in you to shine. Could it be singing a song, telling a joke, leading the conversation, introducing an unusual topic or making a bold statement. Find what feels right for you:

- o Word games (like punning or plays on words).

- o Telling jokes (If you have a hard time remembering good jokes, write them down when you hear one). Start with just one and then build your list.

- o Talk like a writer. Without getting carried away or engaging in deception, add some drama, suspense, pathos or exaggeration. Make your story telling come alive.

- o Gentle teasing (emphasis on gentle and friendly).

- o Flirting (Lots of guidance on the Internet. Easy does it).

- o Inject the unexpected. Surprise yourself, rather than talking about the weather or repeating the same old phrase or story, ask something off-beat, like "What's the happiest moment you can remember from your childhood?" Instead of "How are you?" try "What's the most interesting (outrageous, unusual, etc.) thing that's happened to you in the last X weeks?" Be prepared with your own story to get the ball rolling.

Laughter

Laughter is a uniquely human (and helpful) skill. Do you know how to laugh? That's not meant to be a funny question. Of course, you know the right muscles to use, but do you let yourself laugh, fully and with abandon? Give it a try.

Laughter is highly contagious. One of few sounds that is universally similar across all languages, like the sneeze and the fart. Laughter helps us let out our feelings; it's a gateway to creativity and connection; it cuts through tension and builds connection. Observe any group and one of the first things you're likely to be aware of is, do they laugh or not? It tells you a lot.

Years ago, during the Cold War era, I traveled alone, in Bulgaria, then a brutally repressive, communist dictatorship. Secret police lurked around every corner. Food was scarce, the mood was somber, and I was hungry. No laughing matter.

In Sofia, the capital, I approached a street vendor, a hunched over, scowling old crone, in need of a bath. I pointed at her grill, clearly demonstrating that I'd like to buy some chicken. No response. My next attempt crashed into a sullen sneer followed by a loud, unintelligible expletive. A crowd gathered. A gruff looking guy, in drab, gray garb strutted forward. Secret police? A random terrorist looking for work? I was clueless.

The vendor woman looked like she'd sooner slice and grill me as any of the chickens waiting their turn. The gray garbed thug closed in. I felt his hot breath on my neck. Suddenly, surprising even myself, I clucked. Clucked like a chicken. I clucked and pecked and strutted, becoming my most chicken like self. The old crone ignored my efforts. I clucked louder, now a hungry chicken. She looked at me for the first time. Her sneer slipped, first the forehead, then the eyes, then around the mouth, and finally a smile at the chin. I laughed. She laughed. We beheld each other, two chickens recognizing one another across the barn yard. We laughed together. She flapped her wings. I flapped my wings. She strutted. I strutted. My inner chicken swelled with pride. Other chickens joined us.

The crowd swelled. Soon we were a virtual chicken coop, squawking and flapping and scratching about. No language. Just laughter, a moment that lives in my heart to this day.

Chicken Lady taught me a valuable lesson. A common language is not required for Joyful Connection; the spirit of laughter will do it.

Silence

Silence is shunned in most conversation. We rush in to fill every second with words or actions, whether these add anything or not. We now have texts, and selfies, and breaking news at all times of the day, pings and bongs and distractions of every sort, to rescue us from the momentary awkwardness that silence represents.

Mindful Conversation welcomes silence. Silence creates space for awareness to enter.

By "silence" I mean moment(s) when you don't talk. You do not analyze or judge. You listen and let awareness fill you. When we learn to tolerate silence, we enter a wide meadow, where life, in all its diversity and wonder, can flourish.

If someone is ill or traumatized, we rush in with our words, but the best thing often is just to sit quietly, to be present, to pause for peace. Silence has a magic in it that words often lack.

The conscious practice of silence enables deep listening to oneself and to the world, a chance to hear what life has to say. Maybe the answer is already there. You just have to hear it.

If you are stuck, not knowing quite what to talk about, or what to say about whatever you are talking about, maybe you don't need to say anything. Develop a habit of pausing, taking a moment to consider, then mindfully, allow the conversation to go where it wants to go.

We all know how to be silent. We lack the faith, patience, and courage to allow the body and the ever-active mind to shift from the fearful, controlling self to the trusting, open self.

Three Steps to Play, Laughter, or Silence

When something unusual happens or a conversation seems to stall, most of us rush to the rescue. We follow a 3- step process that often goes like this:

1. Act
2. React
3. Regret

Here's an alternative that can bring lasting change to a conversation or a relationship:

1. **P**ause
2. **R**eflect
3. **A**ct, or remain consciously silent

If helpful, remember the acronym, "PRA." Pronounced like "pray."

1. PAUSE: SLOW DOWN, RELAX.

This is the awareness step, starting point for all things mindful. The challenge is not in the doing, but in the not doing. Did your mother ever tell you to "Stop and count to ten"? What do you do when you are too stressed to function, too distracted to focus, too zoned out to zoom in? *1. Try the Mindful Pause.* Stop. Breathe deeply, slowly, consciously. Pull back from the problem you're engaged with. You can pause anywhere, anytime, whenever you're feeling stressed, rushed, angry, or not thinking clearly. Just breathe. Nothing else. Just breathe.

2. REFLECT: TUNE IN AND ACCEPT WHAT COMES

Set aside judgment, analysis, and critical thinking. Your power lies in noticing and allowing. No matter the thought, feeling or image, just notice and acknowledge it. Let go of any efforts to control. This is a radically different way to take in data from how most of us think – with our critical voice ever ready. "That was stupid ... That was clever ... What an idiot I am." Acknowledge tension or conflict, but don't identify with it or try to overcome it.

If you are in a conversation, experiencing some discomfort or conflict, just watch it. No blame. **Listen to your CP. Just be aware.** Be aware of desire (i.e., to have your way, to tell the funniest joke, to have someone pay attention to you, to "win") then let it go. Your only job is to be present, in the moment, open to discovery.

3. ACT: FOLLOW WHERE THE MOMENT WANTS TO TAKE YOU

Action follows the pause and reflection, but this a different kind of action from the typical rushing around – action for the sake of action. This action is about listening for your own inner voice. Don't make anything happen. Allow the moment to guide you. Surrender into the challenge, into the disappointment, into the opportunity, into the conversation, into life. Let the moment guide you forward.

The point is not to *try* to accomplish anything, but to *allow* the path to emerge. Easier said than done. Most of us want control. We feel safer because we convince ourselves that we can determine the outcome. We think we will get what we want. But control is usually an illusion. We can influence, for sure, but control in most significant matters, is an illusion.

When we welcome what life brings to us, we open to a larger world of possibility. We gain real control by giving up the false illusion of power. Surrender what you can't have, and move into what is possible.

Notes from the Journey

Core Awareness: We gain control by giving it up, surrendering into play, laughter or silence.

Core Value: Awareness. Make space for fresh awareness.

Core Skill: Courage and Patience.

Core Tools: The zipper. Zip your mouth. Wait.

N ext Steps

1. Define the relaxation rituals that help return you to center. For example, conscious breathing (Close your eyes for a second; take two deep breaths; stretch). Give it a try. It may take some practice. Be patient.

2. Choose one of the three basic ways described to put a pause in a conversation: play, laughter, or silence. Commit yourself to trying it out for a week. Take a few moments in the evening to write about your experiment that day. Not to judge it, rather to describe and notice. Then let it be.

Section 2
My Summary and Action Plan

1. **My Points of Awareness / Insights:**

2. **My Potential Implementation Challenges:**

3. **My Action Plan:**

Part 3

The Me - You Conversation: Speak Openly

Chapter 12
Speak so Others Want to Listen

"No, Frank. I'm practicing the Mindful Pause, not the Menopause."

How you speak can make or break a career, a date, a marriage, a friendship, a sale ... or a life. Despite the common desire to talk, many shy away from expressing themselves for fear of appearing foolish, ignorant or "uncool" in some way. Over 30% of people that I have surveyed say that their biggest conversational challenge is "not speaking up frequently or forcefully enough."

The intention in Mindful Conversation is to speak up, to speak openly, about what matters to you, and to speak in a way that others *want* to listen to you.

I was consulting at an urban hospital. The medical chief of staff approached me. "I need your help. It's Dr. Kramer" (not his real name). "Technically he's our best surgeon, but he alienates everyone around him. Several nurses refuse to work with him. We had to postpone a surgery this week because we couldn't staff it."

"What have you tried?" I asked. He shook his head. "I need you to work with him. Please, call him right away."

Dr. Kramer and I met. I tried to convince him of the power of empathy and good listening. I told him of the research of Dr. Helen Reiss[15] at Harvard whose studies of empathy highlighted the power of small, empathic moves – how doctors who simply sit down on a patient's bed receive significantly higher ratings for warmth and caring than their counterparts who stand at bedside. Other research even points to a positive correlation between doctors' empathy scores and rate of patient recovery.

My overtures to Dr. Kramer bombed. "I was here before you came," he told me. "I'll be here after you leave."

I knew that there was something more at stake here, something beyond either of us. If we could touch that something, then real change was possible.

As a last ditch effort, I convinced four brave nurses to meet with Dr. Kramer and me, for a facilitated dialogue. The nurses spoke one by one, openly, without anger or blame, but with passion and conviction about the tension that swirled around the O.R. when Dr. Kramer was working. I asked Dr. Kramer to summarize what he had heard. He started defensively, explaining why the doctor has to be in charge. I intervened. "You don't have to agree with their point of view. Just tell us what you heard them saying." Back and forth we went. "No, that's not exactly it. Let's try again." Slowly the message began to seep in. I asked the nurses if they felt heard. They added examples and more explanation. Finally, with no idea what he might say, I asked Dr. Kramer if he had a point of view he'd like to share. He looked the nurses in the eye, one at a time. "Will you give me another chance?"

When the nurses left, Dr. Kramer looked at me in a way I'd never seen before. "I don't want to be that kind of a doctor," he said. "I don't want to be that kind of a man."

A few well chosen, courageously spoken words can change the world. Dr. Kramer and I never spoke again about that meeting. We worked together for three months. A new buzz around the hospital confirmed that he was, in fact, the best surgeon in town.

Speak Up

There is a time to listen and a time to speak up. By "speak up," I mean sharing your full self – your experiences, your prouds and sorries, your thoughts and feelings, voicing an opinion, taking a stand. Don't just talk about the weather or repeat some worn out story you've told a thousand times. Mindful Speaking is about being authentically present and real in the moment.

By now, hopefully you have a sense of the enormous, life-shifting power of deep listening. And you understand, of course, that conversation is not all about listening. You must also be willing and able to speak effectively, so that others want to listen when you speak.

Core Values of Mindful Speaking

Mindful speaking rises from the same core values of Mindful listening, the C.A.R.E. model: Curiosity, Authenticity, Respect and Empathy. When these values are evident in your speech, others gravitate around, eager to hear what you have to say.

Let's examine each of these characteristics again to understand how it impacts speech.

Curiosity

To be curious in speech means to use the power of your voice continually to push beyond the normal everyday patterns, to discover and explore new worlds. Curiosity calls upon us to reject "confirmation bias," repeating the same old stories and biases from years gone by. Curious speakers absorb how others think and speak, then they zero in on similarities and differences to examine the assumptions, beliefs and experiences; to sharpen and expand their own thinking; learn, grow and connect. Curiosity is the melody for the joyous song of discovery.

Curiosity gives rise to a kind of talk that is the very opposite of serial monologue (Chapter 2). Look at the difference:

1. SERIAL MONOLOGUE

Adrian: "I had Thanksgiving dinner with my sister. It was so disappointing. I made a special pork roast that I was eager to share. She had the tv on as we ate. We might as well have been eating frozen tv dinners. All that work, and no one even noticed the food."

Marsha: "I had Thanksgiving with my husband and his family. We always have Turkey."

You see what is happening here. No connection. No curiosity. Just a grabbing response. Two ships passing in the night.

2. CURIOSITY IN SPEAKING

Adrian: "I had Thanksgiving dinner with my sister. It was so disappointing. I made a special pork roast that I was eager to share. She had the tv on as we ate. We might as well have been eating frozen tv dinners. All that work, and no one even noticed the food."

Marsha: "Pork roast, wow. We always have Turkey. But that must have been so disappointing for you. How did you handle it?"

This brief reply, a combination of reflective response and open-ended question, springs from curiosity. It is an invitation to explore.

An open attitude, reflection plus question = curiosity in action.

Authenticity

We are born with an authenticity meter embedded in our brains. All babies cry when they are unhappy, smile when pleased, and coo when soothed. They quickly learn how to do this. Then they grow up and unlearn what they once knew to make space for more calculated behavior – how to win approval from parents or collect favorable reactions from friends or teachers. Such adaptive behavior is beneficial in some ways, but too often the authenticity meter is tossed into the junk drawer, never to be seen again. We "forget" what was once easy and natural. We lose the authentic self, the voice minus the assumptions, conditioning and beliefs that we wear like hand-me-down clothes that don't fit well.

Authentic speaking gives you and your CP's permission to feel and to express openly. Applying this wisdom in everyday conversation, even if it requires dealing with difficult topics, is the journey of an awakened life.

Being authentic does not mean that you should pour open your heart to everyone, or speak in ways that are mean or hurtful.

Speaking authentically means speaking your truth, admitting doubt when it is present, acknowledging sources if the thought is not your own, and distinguishing what is demonstrable fact, from belief, opinion or assumption. Authentic speaking means feeling your way through conversation as much as thinking. It means staying present in the moment (vs planning what you're going to say while others are speaking). It means ensuring that your gestures, your thoughts, and your words are dancing in sync together. As a grown-up, you may have to relearn what you knew as a small child.

Congruence of Words, Music and Dance

Authenticity requires congruence of verbal and non-verbal messages. This is how we connect and express ourselves powerfully, authentically and fully. Conversation (and dancing) work best when the words, the music and the dance are in sync. But when the speaker's words say one thing (e.g., how happy I am to see you) but the non-verbal message says another (e.g., checking your cell phone instead of making eye contact with your CP).

When words and gestures are in sync, they reinforce one another. When they are at odds, they confuse, undermine trust and confidence. The key is awareness and intention. Be aware of how you are feeling. Be intentional about what verbal and non-verbal message you want to send and what messages you are sending.

Authenticity demands courage. Courage is the choice to speak despite the fear, to know we are traveling beyond our comfort zone and to go there anyway.

Courage comes in different flavors. As Doug Stone and Sheila Heen write in *Difficult Conversations,* "Choosing not to deliver a difficult message is like hanging on to a hand grenade once you've pulled the pin." There is also the courage, and the wisdom, to stay quiet, when now is not the time to speak. Courage does not require one to rush headlong into every burning building. Internal courage is required to back off the need to win every conversation. Choose which battles to engage in and with what words, and which to walk away from. Time and conscious practice nourish both the skills and the courage to use them.

Respect in Word and Gesture

'Respect' is the third value in the C.A.R.E. model. Speaking with respect radically impacts how and if we are heard. Judy approaches her husband Tony who has just finished cleaning up after dinner.

> **Example A, Judy:** "Look how you left the kitchen. You're such a slob." These two sentences are all about blame and judgment. Name calling undermines the person, and almost never changes the behavior. Such language is almost guaranteed to stoke the fires of hostility and resistance in your listener, eliciting a defensive response and damaging the relationship.
> **Example B, Judy:** "I know you did some work to clean up the kitchen, and I appreciate that, but it is still messy. When I come into a messy kitchen, I feel

anxious and annoyed. Would you please finish cleaning up before you leave?" This is a big improvement.
It gives credit where credit may be due; it focuses on
the behavior in question, not the person; it employs an
"I statement" to take responsibility for the speaker's
feelings; it identifies a specific problem, and proposes
a specific action. It moves beyond blame and shame.
The language can still be improved (see Chapter 15),
but it at least has the possibility of understanding and
maybe even healing vs further undermining the relationship.

The point here is that careful choice of words, tone and
gesture make a huge difference. When the three are in sync –
the words, the music and the dance – they are powerful.

Empathy

Empathy, more than any other skill or attitude, is what enables
us to hear the beating heart of another person. Empathy is a
giant antenna, listening for an answer to the question, "What
is life like for you?"

Every conversation regardless of circumstance, topic, or
relationship, whether at home, at work, or at the grocery store,
calls for empathy. You simply cannot connect to others, or
effectively express yourself, if you have no ability or inclination
to understand your CP's feelings, thoughts and desires.
Empathy means having and expressing compassion for all,
yourself included.

Empathy is the pathway to connection, and perhaps the
deepest balm for our fragmented, stressed and lonely world. It
is the tool that enables us to understand, or at least *try* to
understand, what it is like to walk in another's shoes, to think

and feel like another, and to act in support of those with different backgrounds, experiences and belief systems from our own.

Empathy is often confused with sympathy, and perhaps for this reason, viewed by some as a sign of weakness. In fact, empathy, like authenticity, requires emotional courage. Humility and curiosity too. It starts from an assumption of not knowing and a desire to understand the full depth of how someone feels and experiences life. Empathy is the key that unlocks our self-made prisons of loneliness and isolation. It unites us across our common humanity. And, good news: empathy is a learnable, teachable skill.

So how, in the heat of the moment, do you gather your presence sufficiently to choose empathy? The single most powerful tool to help one engage with empathy is the Mindful Pause, discussed in greater detail in Chapter 11.

The Mindful Pause can help you at crucial moments in conversation or in almost any circumstance when you are emotionally wrought, or feeling "triggered" by a strong, negative emotion. (See more detailed discussion of the concept of "emotional triggering" in Part IV, Chapter 20.)

When tension arises, we revert to fast, shallow, unconscious breathing, a physiological response characteristic of the well-known flight-fight-freeze behavior pattern. But such a reaction diminishes oxygen supply to the rational cerebral cortex and makes us the unwitting victim of our more primitive amygdala. The antidote is, unremarkably, slow, deep, conscious breathing. The impact of slowing the breath grounds you in yourself and in the present moment, creating distance between yourself and your ego, space for a more thoughtful response. In short, to engage empathy.

Over and over, I relearn this valuable lesson. When I slow down and ground myself, I emerge from the moment of tension a stronger, more connected, more empathic, and more joyous person. Well worth the wait.

Notes from the Journey

Core Awareness: When the C.A.R.E. values (Curiosity, Authenticity, Respect, Empathy) characterize your speaking, others are drawn in and want to hear what you have to say.

Core Value: Empathy. When we pause and listen deeply enough to grasp another's point of view, then there is far greater likelihood that we will respond with compassion and understanding.

Core Skill: Acknowledge difficulties and tension in conversation; pause anyway.

Core Tool: The Mindful Pause

Next Steps

1. Sometime in the next few days, you are likely to experience a moment of conflict or discomfort in a conversation. It may be mild or severe. Use this moment as an opportunity to experiment. Stay as self-aware as you can. After the experiment, take a few moments to answer these questions. (Writing is often best.)

   A. What specific event or feeling created the tension?

   B. What helped (or stopped) me to slow myself down and try the Mindful Pause?

   C. If you had the presence of mind to try a Mindful Pause, how did it impact your experience of the conversation? Did it impact how you felt about yourself? About your CP? About your relationship?

2. Think about a recent confrontation that you were engaged in (or avoided by not responding.) Imagine yourself at the very first moments of this situation. Imagine going through the three steps of a Mindful Pause. Now re-create the conversation in your mind (better still, on paper). Don't summarize or describe,

but imagine or write out the actual words (as accurately as possible) spoken by yourself and your CP. Reflect on the difference between the conversation as it happened, and how you recreated it after the Mindful Pause experiment.

3. Are there particular people or situations where you think that using the Mindful Pause to guide you into empathy could be helpful? What steps might you take to help remind yourself of this practice when you need it? Define a reward you will give yourself, for when you employ The Mindful Pause in an appropriate situation?

Chapter 13
Speak Openly, from the Heart

"I'm practicing my eye statements, Misha. How am I doing?"

You've taken a Mindful Pause and made the decision to speak in a way that helps you and your CP connect, less competition about who's right and wrong, more moving forward together.

Talking about emotionally charged topics is difficult for most of us. It takes courage, intention and self-discipline. It may require you to expose areas of vulnerability that you'd prefer to keep under wraps. Most importantly, it requires resisting the temptation to blame, judge, criticize, or play gotcha.

Of course, you always have a choice. You can avoid and hide. For a while, you may get away with this, but it is a long, lonely road that most often leads to isolation, alienation and stagnation. Or you can deal with the difficult issues. Often this is not easy, but handled skillfully, it is the path to connection with yourself and others, the glory road to friendship, discovery and continuous learning.

If you aspire to Mindful Conversation, then it's time to talk openly and proudly about what matters to you. Speak your truth from a place of hope and possibility. Never start a conversational segment with, "This is a dumb idea" or "This probably won't work" or "You don't want to hear this." Approach each conversation with the hope of what is possible. "I'm glad to be talking with you about this" or "Let's explore this together and see where it takes us" or "I have an idea. Would you like to hear it?"

Lilly's Story

I had a coaching client, whom I'll call Lilly, a warm, capable, bright woman who found it very hard to express her true self, particularly with her family. Lilly melted at the hint of conflict. The roots of the problem reached back to her childhood, when her parents did little to support her efforts at expression. Sad but not uncommon. As we talked through incident after incident, she began to appreciate the toll that her reluctance to speak up was taking on her self-esteem and confidence. Experimenting with Mindful Conversation attitudes and tools, she began to speak about what she really wanted with her husband. After our initial coaching sessions, she came back brimming with pride. "One of the best conversations we've ever had." I could see it in her eyes, hear it in her voice.

Lilly grew in confidence as she continued to experiment,

with her son and son-in-law, and even her grandson. She noticed that others seemed to respect her more, as she respected herself more. She tracked her successes. She worked on refining her intention, and her role in conversations. She kept a journal and tracked how she felt. Not every time was perfect, but bit by bit she began to get, at a deep level, the power of expressing herself authentically and respectfully, living the C.A.R.E. model.

The Mindful "I" Statement

Expressing oneself openly, especially in conflict situations, can be stressful. "What if I make it worse? What if he gets angry?" With any response, you have a choice to (1) Invite exploration; (2) Oppose exploration; or (3) Ignore. If you want to invite exploration, it may be time to try the "Mindful I Statement."

The original concept of "I Statements" grew out of the work of Carl Rogers (a mentor and hero of mine) and later the Parent Effectiveness Training movement in 1960's.[16] First we'll explore the traditional "I statement," and then the "Mindful I statement."

Let's pick up from the example briefly presented in the last chapter: Judy and her husband Tony. Tony has just done the dishes and cleaned up the kitchen, but in a way that doesn't meet Judy's standards of cleanliness and order. Judy takes a "Mindful Pause" and decides to speak up, to talk about what matters. She is upset, tempted to let her upset dictate her words, as she did in her first example, ("You're a slob. Look how you left the kitchen.") This response was loaded with blame and judgment and led to more defensiveness and acrimony on both sides. Understandable as her feelings may have been, this was not Judy's intent.

Judy's second trial response ("This kitchen is still messy.

Would you please clean it up before you leave?") was better because it resisted name calling, focused on the behavior in question, used respectful language, and proposed a reasonable solution to the problem.

But let's assume that Tony is tired. He doesn't want to talk. He says, "The kitchen is fine. If you want it different, do it. I'm going to watch TV."

Judy recognizes that this is "one of those moments." She tries again. "I'm tired too, and anxious about the kids. You didn't clean up after you ate. I need a clean kitchen ready for the morning. I can't prepare breakfast in this mess. All I ask is that you get the dishes into the dishwasher, put other things away, and wipe down the counter."

If you're not familiar with the term, this is a classic "I statement". She opens with a non-blaming statement of her feeling ("I'm tired too, and anxious about the kids") and its importance to her ("I need to know that we have a clean, orderly kitchen ready for the morning"). She explains the problematic behavior by her CP. ("You didn't clean up after you ate.") And she makes a specific request. ("All I ask is that you get the dishes into the dishwasher, put other things away, and wipe down the counter.") Pretty good, Judy.

But slip into Tony's shoes. How might he respond now? How might this shift in language impact how he feels and what he might say or do? What is the likelihood of some behavioral change now?

Judy has had a chance to air her feelings, and this exchange has far greater likelihood of producing some understanding and resolution of the tension between Judy and Tony without damaging the relationship.

The "Mindful I statement" builds on a good tool and makes it even stronger. Use of I statements can sound formulaic and wooden, the same problem as with active listening, more like a downloaded app than talk from the heart. Rather than dictating specific language, the Mindful I Statement is based in the C.A.R.E. model.

1. It is grounded in non-judgmental, empathic listening. (Respect)

2. Rather than using a formulaic language, the speaker uses his / her own wording and phrases, following a set of mindfulness principles. (Authenticity)

3. The speaker names and accepts responsibility for his / her own feelings and requests. (Authenticity)

4. The language is present tense focused and specific to this incident rather than global. (Empathy)

5. The "ask" proposes joint problem solving, responsibility and action. (Respect)

How might Judy incorporate these principles? Let me reiterate, no formula or specific wording can guarantee success. What is important is to find the tone and language that fits the message, your personal style of speech, and is true to the C.A.R.E. principles. For example, Judy might say, "Tony, I know how hard you work, and I appreciate all you do to keep us strong financially. That's so vital to our well-being. I've been working hard too. I feel anxious right now, with one sick child and one struggling at school, so it's doubly important to me that we have cleanliness and order at home. I want to work this out together. We've agreed that it's fair for you to do the after dinner clean-up while I get the kids ready for bed. I need to have the kitchen ready for morning. And you're right, I do have some very specific standards that are important to me. Can we talk about this, explore how we can both get our needs met?"

Can you hear the difference between the two conversations?

o Mindful I statements stay in the present tense, avoiding reference to past problem areas ("You left the same kind of mess *last week")* and general accusations ("You *always* leave a mess in the kitchen. As usual, you didn't clean up after you ate").

o Mindful I statements use "feeling language" rather than "identity language." Rather than "I am anxious" she says, *"I feel anxious."* This small shift acknowledges that it is a feeling, not a state of being. Feelings change, and this one will too.

o As opposed to blaming ("You make me so mad") the speaker names and takes responsibility for his/her own feelings and requests. *"I feel anxious ... And you're right, I do have some very specific standards that are important to me."*

o Mindful I statements support feelings with clear examples, behavior and data when available – *"one sick child and one struggling at school."*

o Mindful I statements include empathic expressions that demonstrate the speaker's understanding of the situation and feelings. *"Tony, I know you work hard. I appreciate all you do to keep the family strong financially. That's so vital to our well-being."*

o Mindful I statements refer to specific, actionable behavior, in which one or both parties have clear control. *"To sleep well at night and be ready to get the kids off to school, I need to have the kitchen ready for morning."*

o Rather than demanding a particular response, Mindful I statements explicitly invite the CP's to engage together to explore the topic at hand. "Can we talk about this together, how to get both our needs met?"

o Mindful I statements use respectful language, naming ("Tony, I know how hard you work") rather than name calling (*"You're a slob"*).

Please don't be overwhelmed by such a list. Let the C.A.R.E. model guide you. Make the language your own, coming from your heart, and the words will be right.

The Connection Opportunity

Every conversation is an opportunity to connect. Conflicts, though stressful, present a unique opportunity to deepen a relationship. If they are handled well. The opportunity will not seize you. You have to claim it.

The use of Mindful I statements does not guarantee success. Nothing can, but it significantly lowers the risk of doing harm.

Time now to have some fun.

Notes from the Journey

Core Awareness: Emotionally charged conversations are a risk and an opportunity.

Core Value: Empathy. In speech and in listening.

Core Skill: Resisting the urge to "win" the conversation.

Core Tool: Mindful I Statement.

Next Steps

1. Think about a recent conflict situation that you were engaged in (or avoided by not responding.) In your conversational journal, write out a Mindful I statement that comes from your heart.

2. Opportunities to practice Mindful I statements will occur. Practice even with a small inconvenience. Don't worry about doing it perfectly. Study the principles and follow the C.A.R.E. model. What's important is to begin. Reflect and learn.

Chapter 14
Conversational Play

"Wanna build a sandcastle together?"

I sat for three years on a remote mountaintop in Germany.

But not in meditation. While in the Air Force, I was the Communications Officer for a radar site on the East German border. Mostly it was quiet, but occasionally an emergency, like when the entire switchboard (back when there were switchboards) died and stayed dead for 3 days. A lot of people were upset. With me.

Managing the antiquated cable system, originally built by the Nazis in WW II, was part of my job. During the outage, and after about 30 sleepless hours, I was in worse shape than the switchboard. I had to go home to sleep. Wanting to appear conscientious and supportive, I told my sergeant, "If anything changes, *anything,* call me right away."

The sergeant, a hard-working, good man, paused and looked at me the way you might eye a dog who's just pooped on your expensive rug. "But, sir," he said, "how ... can ... should I call you?"

No switchboard = no call, in or out.

For weeks, I carried around a sack of embarrassment about how stupid I must have appeared. I was, after all, the Communications Officer. Then I began to see the humor in the situation. Now it's one of my favorite stories.

Conversation is often humorous, when we don't get in our own way of seeing the humor. The common enemies of conversational fun are perfectionism, judgmentalism, stress, and "frozen popsicle-ism," a term I just coined that means staying frozen inside your own self-made ice chest.

So, one of the strategies toward play and humor is **inviting in the absurd.** In the realm of the ordinary, the absurd is never far from view. And it can be very funny.

Dick and Jane

On a rainy day in April.

Jane: "Let's go for a walk today."

Dick: "It's pouring. We'll get soaked."

This response is logical and ordinary. OK, but not especially fun.

Jane: "Let's go for a walk today."

Dick: "On a beautiful day like this? Sure. And how about we jump off the nearest bridge for some extra fun?"

This response is full of sarcasm. Sarcasm, particularly when it is aimed at someone else, is a lightly disguised putdown. Mostly disrespectful. Also not amusing.

Jane: "Let's go for a walk today."

Dick: "Shall I wear my scuba gear or my new polka-dot pants, the ones that look like rain drops all over."

Well, he's trying at least. Maybe you find it funny. Maybe not. At a minimum, it breaks the tension and it's not a put down. Dick is dropping into the puddle of the absurd, the home of a lot of fun and humor.

Conversation as Play

Let's start in the decidedly unfunny realm of fear. If you approach conversation as a contest, then you consistently will *struggle* to win. If you focus your attention on protecting yourself from rejection or trying to impress the world, then you are constantly on trial. But if you approach conversation as a source of joy like play, then you're open for fun, and you're likely to find it. And more joyous relationships along the way. When you become the kind of person who welcomes fun and play, then you become the kind of person that others want to be around. You don't have to choose between being serious and having fun. In fact, the two work well together.

This chapter is not about how to be a stand-up comic. Or tell jokes. Both are fine in their place, but both are, in fact, performances, mostly canned, programmed humor. Play is about letting go and allowing something unexpected to emerge. You can't force it or memorize it or schedule it. But you can get out of the way and welcome it. As an exchange program[17] I participated in, put it, 'Expect the unexpected.'

When we think of conversation as play rather than as competition or performance, then we ask a different kind of question: Not "How can I win?" but "How can we enjoy?" Not "How can I look good?" but "How can we have fun with this?" The spirit of play is about letting go rather than holding on, allowing rather than forcing, being vulnerable rather than controlling. Play is the language of children. You knew it once. Invite it back in by not walling it out.

Surrendering into Play

We've talked about vulnerability. A willingness to be vulnerable is a pre-requisite for authentic conversational play, but many people are not willing (or able) to take that leap of faith. If you are struggling to hide your own insecurities, trying to impress the world, then mindful fun may not be the path. Vulnerability is the key that unlocks the door. Prerequisites are a willingness to make fun of yourself and a desire to break out of the box, to discard norms of expression and be present, really present, to the moment.

If this sounds like fun and a worthwhile experiment, then let's go forward.

The basic, three step model to fun in conversation, goes like this. Spoiler Alert: It's a paradox. You gotta:

1. Want it

2. Wait for it

3. Welcome it when it comes

Step 1. Want it. Well, do you?

Step 2. Wait for it, is perhaps the easiest to explain and hardest to follow. It goes like this:

That's right. Blank, open, empty. Because in many ways, you need only to be open and allow. You can follow the above three steps in any order, because whichever order you choose will be wrong. That's right; it's wrong. Your job is to laugh with abandon at yourself for trying. And then tell the story about how you tried and floundered. Your failure becomes your success.

Are you ready? No one ever is.

Humor and Play

The humor that we're exploring here is the spontaneous stuff that comes out of who you are, whom you're with, and the situations and humorous circumstances that swirl around you, day in and out, noticed or unnoticed. Once you realize that failure can be an unplanned path to success, you have nothing to fear but boredom itself.

The cardinal rule of conversational humor is to laugh at yourself, never at someone else. Ronald Reagan built a very successful career around self-deprecating humor. As president, he made fun of his age and tendency to nod off. "I have left orders to be awakened at any time in case of national emergency – even if I'm in a Cabinet meeting." Perhaps his best moment in the campaign of 1984 was his pledge, made during a debate with his considerably younger opponent, Walter Mondale. "I will not make age an issue of this campaign. I am not going to exploit, for political purposes, my opponent's youth and inexperience." In twenty-four words, with a smile and without acrimony or name calling, Reagan undermined Mondale's efforts to portray him as too old for the job. No wonder he was often referred to as "the great communicator." Self-deprecating humor makes you human. And likable. And the rest is history.

There's a big difference between "self-deprecating" and "self- critical." "Self-deprecating" acknowledges our common humanity and frailty. It announces, "We're all swimming in the soup together, so let's have fun."

Critical: "I am such an idiot. I wasted 45 minutes trying to order that gift online, and then I ordered the wrong thing. I'll never get it right. A three-year-old could have done better than I did."

Self-deprecating: "I wasted 45 minutes trying to order that gift online. I couldn't remember whether I'd used an exclamation point or a $ sign in the password. I must have 50 passwords. By the time I got registered with a new password, I'd forgotten what I wanted to buy."

The critical example uses name calling ("such an idiot") and comparison ("a three-year-old could ..."), both of which laugh at rather than with. The speaker catastrophizes the problem ("I'll never get it right"). The "humor" has little to do with the behavior, but rather it diminishes the speaker. Such talk often makes others feel awkward. Self-derogatory humor is a lose-lose proposition.

Self-deprecating humor, by contrast, can actually enhance

self-acceptance. It is an act of vulnerability, a sign of strength and confidence, and an illustration of how we all mess up because we're all human. The deeper message is, "I'm not perfect, but I do the best I can, and I'm ok with my faults."

My mother, like me, had a penchant for getting down on herself. She'd often say, "Nobody likes me, everybody hates me. I'm going out in the garden to eat worms." This is obviously not literally true. It is self-deprecating humor and connects us by exaggerating our common human foible, to feel sorry for ourselves.

Humor is an art and a style. It comes easier to some than others, but if it's something you want to develop, you can. Hold the intention. Let go of the struggle. Allow it. Look for humor in everyday events. If you're going out for an errand, find at least one humorous circumstance. It doesn't have to be rolling-in-the-aisles funny. Slightly quirky, curious, odd, campy, pleasing, lively, entertaining, or slippery will do fine. You may have to modify some aspect of it, or exaggerate slightly. That's fine, too. We're searching for fun. Practice by telling the story to someone within 24 hours. Tell it poker faced or with a smile, in whispers or dramatically. Draw out the fun.

Learning to Play

Play and humor are cousins. Both should be fun. Play comes naturally to most children, but many of us forget how. We grow up and become "serious." Mindful Conversation is a serious subject, but that doesn't mean that it must always be serious.

Being playful, like being authentic, sounds like it should be the easiest thing in the world. For many of us, it's not. Particularly if you feel serious, lonely, hurt, unappreciated, an outsider, or withdrawn, then being playful may feel almost impossible.

Mindful Conversation does not require you to change who you are. It invites you to include parts of yourself that you may have lost in the shuffle.

If this idea appeals, the single most important step is committing to change – knowing why you want to do it, and sticking with it, even if you don't get immediate results. Identify other people or topics that arouse the playful spirit in you. Try new approaches to familiar routine – just for the fun of it. For example, if you always sleep in the same bed, experiment with a new location. Try a night out under the stars, or throw a mattress on the floor in the living room – just to play around, see what it's like. Change your location at the dinner table, and notice how it's different. Then talk about the experiment. Share and show whatever feelings you had.

Go Forth and Play

Find the directions to your playground. Play is one of the very best ways to meet and love ourselves and others. You are playing when you let down your guard, forget the stresses, forget about accomplishing goals or impressing anyone, and relax into your true self. Life is so short. Why not have some fun?

Conversation is a built-in sandbox. Bring your toys. Connect. Express. Thrive. And learn how to tell a good story (next up).

Notes from the Journey

Core Awareness: Humor and play are essential parts of conversation experiences.

Core Value: Curiosity and Courage. Play requires adults to stretch back into childhood, beyond the normal comfort zone.

Core Skill: Letting go of the need for control, predictability, certainty.

Core Tool: Smile.

Next Steps

1. Social conversation should be fun. If none of the strategies in this chapter appeal, don't take it too seriously. What would make it fun for you?

2. How can you give yourself permission to play? Set aside 10 minutes each day to either do nothing or to play.

3. Identify 3 people and 3 situations that make you laugh. Now that you have these two lists, what are you going to do with them?

Chapter 15
Tell Me a Story!

It was a dark and stormy night, and the Captain said to his mate, "I never learned how to tell a good story, so I don't know what to say on a dark and stormy night. Do you have any ideas?"

The Power of Story

Since the time when the first cave men and women grunted at one other across the fire, we have been story tellers. A good story, well told, captures our attention, and connects us across whatever barriers may exist. Stories connect people to people and people to ideas. Facts and figures, charts and graphs appeal to the logical brain. Stories speak to the heart. Stories engage, motivate and inspire.

Effective stories are actively use both verbal and non-verbal language. A good story engages others emotionally about a topic of mutual interest, curiosity or experience.

A good story draws us into the characters and the action. It makes us feel: laugh or cry, be scared or calmed, love or fear. You see yourself, somewhere, somehow, inside the story. You have most likely never bought chicken from a vendor in Bulgaria. But perhaps you enjoyed my chicken vendor story from Bulgaria (Chapter 11), partly because you too have been an outsider. You know the feeling, and that's enough.

A good storyteller is welcome anywhere – at work, at home, on a date, or in casual conversation. Some come to storytelling naturally, but many of us don't. No matter, it's a learnable skill. When you hear a good storyteller it sounds so simple, but it takes practice, a bit like learning to play a musical instrument. Once you've got it, you will burst with pride as you spread joy and learning around you.

The Elements of Story

Typically a story has a beginning, a middle, and an end. The **beginning** grabs the attention of the listener. It can be provocative, or suspenseful, or just sweet. It can be a question, a challenge or a promise. It can be humorous or frightening, but the best story openings engage us emotionally. My Bulgarian story has a dark opening. I wanted to create a feeling of suspense and fear. I could have said, "Traveling for westerners in communist countries during the Cold War was dangerous." That's factual, pertinent, and instructive, but also flat and unengaging. Instead, I chose, "Secret police lurked around every corner. Food was scarce, the mood was somber, and I was hungry." I wanted you to worry, to suffer a bit, as I had. When we *feel*, then we're engaged, often without being aware of why. We learn without realizing we're being taught. Magic starts to happen.

The **middle** of a story usually involves a conflict, tension, suspense or humor of some kind. Usually something is not right. All the elements of good fiction writing are at play here: character, plot, setting, theme, imagery, dialogue, etc. The trick is to choose which ones are essential to advance the effect you intend. You don't want to drag out the story and lose your audience. Generally speaking, a good conversational story lasts no longer than 2 - 3 minutes. You must keep the story moving forward towards your conclusion in an engaging way.

Language is important. Use strong words (especially verbs and nouns) and images: "I was afraid" states a fact, quickly forgotten. "I cowered in the corner like a frightened puppy" shows an image that pierces the armor. Use sensual language (what you can see, hear, taste, smell, or feel by touch). Choose your words carefully. "I walked slowly" tells it; "I stumbled over the rubble" shows it through use of a strong verb (stumbles) and noun (rubble).

The intangible aspect of the middle, and often the most important aspect of your storytelling, is the **quality and tone** of your voice, facial expression, and body language. This may not show up on the written page, but in conversation, it is the star. And it should be. Demonstrate the **emotion** you want to convey in every word and gesture. Your voice should employ volume (loud to soft), pitch (high to low), speed (fast to slow) and tone (happy, sad, relaxed, frightened, etc.). Your face and body language (hand gestures, smiles and frowns, rolling eyes or pouting lips, movements, posture) will live on long after your words are forgotten. Storytelling is no time for a flat, lifeless monotone. You have to believe in your own story and inject energy into the telling. When you tell a story, you are choosing to take center stage, no time to hide in the corner.

If the above list intimidates you, worry not. What you most need is to <u>feel</u> the truth of your story (the excitement, the fear, the hope ...). Much of the rest will take care of itself.

The **end** of the story usually brings some kind of resolution or reflection on the tension created earlier. Generally, keep the ending short and pithy. A line of dialogue may do it, or a simple statement of the resolution.

The implication of all of the above can be summarized by one word: practice. A mediocre story told well can be a great hit. A great story told poorly is generally a flop. You will not magically become a good storyteller without practice. Practice by yourself (in front of a mirror, into a recording device); practice with others (first in non-challenging situations, with one other person). If you are really serious, find a coach or a class or join toastmasters, listen to the many great storytellers on the Internet (This American Life, The Moth, Radio Hour). Ask for feedback. Work at it. Have fun.

And if all of this sounds overwhelming, there are just two things that really stand out: your first sentence and your last. Nail them and you're home free.

What to Talk About

"I don't have any stories to tell." Students in my classes tell me this all the time. Not true. You just don't recognize the stories that lie within you.

The list of possible topics is infinite. Here are a few random prompts:

o   Memorable childhood moments.

o   Mistakes you've made and lessons learned.

o   Accidents and Mishaps.

- o Coincidences / Planning / Spontaneity.

- o Falling in love. Falling out of love.

- o What I'm grateful for. Pet peeves.

- o Saving face.

- o Learning to say "no." Learning to say "yes."

- o Challenges of Technology / Parenting / Dating / Friendship / etc.

You can tell a story about anything. The real question is "What interests you? What matters? What would you enjoy telling a story about?"

The subject matter that interests you most is the story you should tell. Connection is the most basic goal of Mindful Conversation. Storytelling is a great tool to help you connect to yourself and to others. Telling a story about what genuinely interests you (or discovering what that is if you're not sure) is the most direct route to yourself. Storytelling can make you come alive. Allow yourself to feel the story. Reveal yourself deeply and you inevitably touch universal themes. Which connect you, of course, directly with others.

Start thinking in terms of story. A story can be tiny (a leaf you saw fall from a tree, a gesture you witnessed) or it can be about a life changing event. Stories can be about yourself or another (but should never make fun of or demean another). Personal experiences, particularly if you are willing to show your own vulnerabilities, are the heart of fine story telling. Being willing to laugh at yourself is a great starting place.

A good story often connects to some higher value or principle, stated or not. You may not even know what that principle is until you tell the story for the first time.

Practice by yourself. Practice on anyone who will listen. Ask or feedback. If you "failed," try again and "fail better." Write down your stories. Experiment.

When the Story's done

Don't drag the story on interminably and lose your audience. The last step in conversational storytelling is to vacate center stage and transition smoothly back into conversation mode. Sometimes this will happen automatically. People will pick up on your themes and make comments, tell their own stories, or ask questions.

A great way to engage your audience is the subject for the next chapter, asking a pertinent question that explicitly invites others into the topic. For example, if I'd just finished telling my Bulgarian story, I might ask a question such as, "Have you ever had a memorable connection with a stranger? How did it come about?" or "Have you ever used unusual techniques to talk with someone when there was no common language?" or "What would you have done in my situation?" Such questions create a great transition and invite others into the storytelling ring. They promote connection and the realization that we're all in this together.

Notes from the Journey

Core Awareness: The power of effective storytelling – to connect, motivate, influence and inspire.

Core Value: Respect. Stories are not gossip. Use language that is respectful of yourself and others.

Core Skill: Enthusiasm. Invite your emotions into your story telling. Show your joy, or your sadness.

Core Tools: The Delay. Hint at what might be coming, but don't reveal it right away. Keep your audience in suspense, for a bit. Fulfill your promises, but not until you've made your audience eager.

Next Steps

1. Create a story right now. About something you've experienced in the last couple of days. If nothing comes to mind, then tell a story about your reaction to this chapter and the idea of becoming a storyteller. Begin by talking about it, out loud, to yourself. Record yourself. Play with the idea. Have fun with it.

2. Develop at least one story idea to the point where you're prepared to present it to someone. Within the next week, find (or create) an opportunity to tell your story.

3. Bring up the idea of storytelling in conversation with someone. Discuss what is easy and what is a challenge for you. Ask your CP about their experience.

4. Define one (or two) important values that you hold. Develop a story that illustrates a time when you lived true (or not true) to the value. Include something about the impact of following (or not following) your own best advice.

Chapter 16
Ask. The Power of Questions

"So, George, you and our daughter are spending time together. Let's cut to the chase. Here is a list of questions covering education, upbringing, life goals, achievements, financial stability, family intentions, recreational pursuits, emotional intelligence, and sexual history. We'd appreciate your answers in writing. How does next Thursday sound?"

Asking the right question at the right time opens the door to real connection. Which questions you ask others shifts the conversation, the depth and nature of your relationships. Which questions you ask yourself impacts how you think and act. Not asking questions generally guarantees one-way conversations, where ego and competition for air time dominate, instead of connection and discovery.

Learning to ask great questions is a master skill, essential to Mindful Conversation. Questions inspire creativity and innovation. Skillful questions are the pathway to truth and learning. Research of thousands of top business executives found that the most creative, successful business leaders are usually the ones who ask the best questions.

The owner of a hotel had received many complaints that the elevators were too slow. He consulted an elevator company. The price tag for a new elevator was prohibitive. He bemoaned his problem to a friend.

"Let me poke around," the friend suggested. "Ask a few questions. If I come up with a solution that you like and that solves the problem, you pay me 10% of what I save you."

A week later, the friend called back. "I think I have a solution."

"What's it cost?" the owner asked skeptically.

"About $500."

The owner smirked. "What? Helium balloons?"

"I asked your guests one question: 'Can you describe your experience waiting for the elevators?'

"'We wait,' they said. 'And wait. Big waste of time. I wouldn't stay at this hotel again.' Then I observed guests at a nearby hotel," the friend continued. "The guests there wait too, at times just as long as the guests at your hotel, but they wait happily." He paused, long enough to let the distinction sink in. "That hotel has mirrors all around the elevators. The guests check out their clothes, smooth their hair ... and barely notice the wait."

"So your solution is ...?" the owner inquired.

"Mirrors," the friend said.

Mirrors it was. The complaints ended. The questioner earned a nice commission, not bad remuneration for asking one question. A good question. The right question.

Barriers to Asking

Asking good questions requires thought. Questions are birthed in curiosity. (The "C" in C.A.R.E.) Too many people fear that questions spotlight their ignorance or naiveté. *I'd like to ask about ... but I might sound stupid.* Asking questions is the breakfast of champions. Avoid asking and you are choosing to starve while you strut about in intellectual arrogance or ignorance, missing the opportunity for growth and learning.

Many people don't inquire because they have just one subject of interest: me, me, me. Good questioners play on a much larger field. They are interested in others. Interested in the life around them.

Good questions involve genuine inquiry, seeking to understand what makes someone or something tick. Inquiry doesn't mean asking someone you've just met to tell you about their innermost secrets. Nor does it mean showing off your superior wisdom, or finding fault in their story.

When you practice the art of inquiry, you share the joy of being a modern-day Will Rogers, who said, "I never met a man I didn't like." Open wide your curiosity, and you'll discover interesting, likeable people everywhere. You'll enjoy them more, and they, in turn, are more likely to want to hear what you have to say. (There are exceptions, of course. Some people simply never have and never will be interested in anything beyond their own ego. Their loss.)

Warren Berger, journalist and author, has built a career studying the world of questions and questioners. He explores why our institutions don't do more to encourage the practice of questioning. In his fine exploration of the topic, *A More Beautiful Question*, he writes, "Questions challenge authority and disrupt established structures ... forcing people to *think* about doing something differently." Think about doing something differently, how awkward!

For the love of Curiosity

Questions are the magic link between listening and speaking. Discover new ideas, hear new stories, expand your world. Questions are the secret sauce for conversation, even with people you know well. Question yourself too. You may meet someone you'd enjoy knowing better.

Everyone has a story to tell. Most people love telling their story, but often they need an invitation – your questions. People drop clues about what they'd like to talk about. Make it your job to see what you can discover or understand. Invite others to shine, and they will love you forever. Be a miner. Search for the vein that unlocks the gold that lies waiting.

Types of Questions

Generally, we choose our conversational questions spontaneously and without much advance preparation. That can work well. But those who inquire for a living (lawyers, doctors, journalists, scientists, leaders, teachers, etc.) often prepare their questions in advance.

Beyond basic fact finding (Who, What, When, Where type inquiries), most questions fall into three categories:

1. **Connecting Questions** - where the primary purpose is to connect, enjoy or explore some subject of interest. These questions are likely to be open ended, with space for the respondent to take the question in different directions.

   Example: "Sounds like you've been to a lot of interesting places. Are there particular ones that are most memorable for you?"

2. **Influencing Questions** - in which the primary purpose is to teach or influence another. These questions are more narrowly focused, probing and investigative.

   Example: "So you're having a hard time talking with your daughter. So much depends on circumstance and relationship. I'm curious what you've tried. When do you talk? About what? How do you approach her?"

3. **Problem Solving Questions** - the primary purpose is to respond to some problem, condition or opportunity that requires attention.

   Example: "You're trying to find a good used car. Have you carefully defined your criteria for the car you really want?"

Find the Child in You

Young children are incessant questioners. *Why is the sky blue? Why is it light in the morning?* Why? Why? Why? It's tempting to say, "Stop asking so many questions." A better response is, "You ask such great questions. Let's explore that together."

Children ask questions because their curiosity meter is wide open. Most children are great questioners at age 4, but they've lost this instinct by the time they reach 14, when curiosity has been replaced by the desire to appear cool.

How can we recover the innocence that opens us to wonder? Studying young children reveals clues. Research shows that as soon as children enter preschool, many begin to cut back on their questioning. Some preschools are already hard at work, filling the minds of children with facts and answers to questions that they never asked. Disengaged and spoon-fed, these children close down the wonder machine, replacing "why" with "So what?" and "That's stupid." They stop asking questions, become passive, couch potatoes vs explorers, consumers vs creators, parrots vs artists. Is this the foundation for a vibrant, learning, diverse democracy? Our schools and our adult role models must do better.

What if we ask the children to identify and refine the questions that interest them? What if these questions then become the basis of their curriculum? What if the parent / teacher role is redefined as helping children to explore the questions that interest them most? Some innovative schools and organizations are working on exactly such an approach. The Right Question Institute[18] in Boston, for example, focuses on building people's skills so children (and adults) know how to ask better questions, participate in decisions that affect them and advocate for themselves. When you learn to love the questions as much as the answers, then you are on the road to wisdom.

Here are a few thought starters for putting questions at the center of your conversation:

1. Speak openly and often about the power and fun of asking questions. Validate others who ask questions. "You ask such great questions. I really enjoy that."

2. Ask questions about questions. For example, for any topic that you are studying or discussing, stop and ask, "What are the most interesting questions we might ask about this topic? What would you like to learn?" Then, "How might we go about answering these questions?"

3. When children come home from school or at the dinner table, instead of asking content focused

questions (e.g., "How was your day at school?" (So often a dead end question.) ask process oriented questions (e.g., "What would you like to talk about at dinner tonight? How about if we each suggest one topic?" "Let's share news of our day. Who wants to go first?")

Integrate Better Questions into your Conversation.

Every conversation is a treasure hunt. Your CP has something interesting to say. It's your job to uncover it, to ask the right question and listen in a way that reinforces your interest in what they have to say. Asking questions requires intention.

Inquire, not as a prosecutor, trying to establish blame or to put someone on the spot, but to uncover new worlds, to learn and expand, to invite someone else to talk about what is important to them.

Much of the typical advice about questioning touts the advantages of open-ended questions. (Questions that cannot be answered with a simple "yes" or "no.") My observation is that the actual wording of the question is often less important than the intention behind it. Intention shows up in eye contact, tone of voice, volume, emphasis, body language, facial expression. We "hear" these messages even louder than we hear the words you use. If these signals telegraph your genuine interest, then less elegantly worded questions work fine.

That said, if you're going to an event where you don't know people or feel uneasy, preparing possible questions in advance may boost your confidence. Practice at home with a mirror or recorder. If you're going to a party after a concert, an obvious starting ground is "Did you enjoy the concert?

What did you enjoy most about it? Anything you didn't like?" This may be all that's required. Be ready with follow up questions like, "What thoughts went through your mind as you were listening? If you were X's manager and coaching them on how to put on the best show possible, what would you advise? Do you ever fantasize performing on stage? If you were to learn an instrument (or if you already have) what instrument did you / would you choose? If you were an instrument, what instrument would you be?"

Every circumstance has its own set of discovery questions. At a PTA meeting, ask about another's relationship to the school or PTA. "What grades are your children in? Are you satisfied with your children's experience here? Any teachers you particularly like?" To go deeper, try questions like, "Is this school anything like the school you went to? How is it different? How do you think education has changed for the better? For the worse?

What attitudes and skills do you think kids are going to most need in the future?"

For almost any social gathering, here's a question that I love to play with. "Is there any question that you wish some-one would ask you?" I've tried this one at many gatherings.

Sometimes it earns a bit of a startled response. One CP said, "Wow, what a question. You have a unique mind." I smiled. Another meandered about a bit, then told me about her ability to jump across two kinds of time, linear and fluid time and how she's had this ability since childhood, but never told people about it. If you want to dare BIG, try something like, "What event (person / activity) made you who you are today?" Be judicious. If you feel confident of yours and your CP's desire to dig deeper, how about "What would you do if you weren't afraid?" Such questions aren't always appropriate. On the other hand, many people wish for more personal conversations but don't know how to make them happen.

If you're probing into a difficult subject, or if someone is stressed, rather than asking a direct question, ask if they'd like to talk about the topic. It's softer, more inviting, less demanding. To someone who's been sick, rather than "How are you feeling today?" Try "Would you like to talk about how you're feeling?"

Homage to Questions

Are you asking questions? What kind of questions? Are you using questions wisely, using them to open the doors of wonder, to deepen your connection to others and to help others to explore and express? We live in a time in which extremism and divisiveness have become the norm. Loud is mistaken for true; misinformation dominates the air waves; demonizing those who are different is the meat of unscrupulous politicians and media pundits. In this toxic environment, quiet, empathic inquiry stands out like a beautiful flower in a wasteland. Some call it political correctness. I call it human caring. Sincere questioning in combination with reflective listening is the royal road to friendship and learning.

Homage to a Great Questioner

I'll close this chapter with a word of homage to a writing colleague, the late Will Wise, author of *Ask Powerful Questions: Create Conversations That Matter*. Will has lots of useful information on the subject. For a burst of joy, take some time right now, and consider your answers to Will's 3 favorite questions: [19]

1. What brings you joy?

2. What is this moment teaching you right now?

3. What is a crossroads you are at?

Notes from the Journey

Core Awareness: Learning to ask the right question may be a bigger leap towards fulfillment and success than a wall of diplomas.

Core Value: Curiosity. Open the door of curiosity. See what's hiding behind it. Sometimes the most naive questions open the biggest doors.

Core Skill: Using questions to gain understanding and to demonstrate interest and empathy.

Core Tool: Ask and then be quiet. Create space for the answer. Listen to the answer, then ask follow-up questions. Don't stop until you are satisfied.

Next Steps

1. What kind of questioner are you? Willing? Eager? Reluctant? Shy? Review the common barriers to questioning and write an exploratory piece in your conversational journal about what blocks you from asking more questions. Follow up with a piece on how you might best overcome your barriers.

2. Before a date with a friend, think in advance of one probing, imaginative question (or topic) that you'd like to explore. Commit yourself to working it in to the conversation.

3. If you are going to a party or gathering where you may be in contact with people that you don't know, try out the exploratory questions suggested in this chapter ("Is there any question that you wish someone would ask you? Or a special topic that you'd most like to talk about?") Be brave. What's the worst that could happen? What's the best that could happen? Write in your journal about what actually happens and how you feel about yourself for having tried.

Chapter 17
The 7 Deadly "Sins" of Conversation

*"I've been trying to talk my way out of here for centuries.
It's been hellish. Maybe I'll try listening."*

Conversation can, and should, be a very positive activity. But all of us develop unconscious habits that become annoying to our listeners. Trimming your conversation of such habits will vastly improve your communication and motivate others to want to listen to you. This chapter outlines seven such common "habits" (that all of us indulge from time to time) that we can reduce or eliminate with some focused attention.

Brain research[20] indicates that some of these annoying habits increase the flow of endorphins to the brain. They may supply temporary relief from stress and anxiety, may even provide short term satisfaction and the illusion of control. But you pay a steep price.

As you read through the list of "sins," score yourself, in terms of how often you "sin" in this way:

If you do this **NEVER,** give yourself **ZERO** points.
If you do this **SELDOM** give yourself **ONE** point.
If you do this **SOMETIMES,** give yourself **TWO** points.
If you do this **OFTEN,** give yourself **THREE** points.
Here is your personal score card:

Behavior	Title	My Score
1	The Me-Me-Me'er	
2	The Unwanted Advisor	
3	The Avoider	
4	The Interrupter	
5	The Non-Listener	
6	The Wanderer	
7	The Puppet	
	Total Score	

1. THE ME-ME-ME'ER

The world is filled with people who talk about "me, myself, and nothing but myself." Endlessly. They show little, often no, interest in others.

There is nothing wrong with talking about yourself. The problem arises when that is the dominant topic you talk about, often with no sense of time, your CP's interest or desires also to talk.

Like everyone, Me-Me-Me'ers want to express and connect. But they don't know how. They are unskilled or unmotivated in how to listen to others, how to inquire, or how to discuss ideas outside their own, immediate experience.

205

Overcoming the temptation to indulge in endless self-talk starts with awareness of the problem and moves on to expressed curiosity about whomever or whatever you are curious about. First, awareness. Notice how much of your time you spend talking about yourself. How many of your sentences start with "I"? This is not to disparage self-revelation and self-reflection, such as "What are my strengths and weaknesses? How can I improve myself?" Self-inquiry is very different from self-absorption (Aren't I smart? Beautiful? Talented? Or, I am too fat, thin, tall, short, poor, neurotic, etc.)

Develop a list of 3 topics you'd like to talk about other than yourself. See if you can conduct a conversation for 3 minutes without saying the word "I." Extend the time. Learn how to connect with others by listening deeply to their stories. Learn how to ask questions to draw others out. You'll be glad you did. And so will your friends.

2. THE UNINVITED ADVISOR

As soon as you mention the hint of a problem, the Uninvited Advisor jumps in with advice on how to solve it. No need (or time) to understand the problem, the why or how behind it.

It's so much easier to solve other people's problems than your own. Unrequested advice usually does more harm than good. It creates resistance and blocks the development of deeper understanding. It also does nothing to empower the receiver. Rather it says, "You can't solve your own problems, but I can." Untrue and demeaning.

My advice on advice giving is simple: don't ... unless it is requested or specifically contracted for. To follow this principle requires strong mindful intention. If you really want to help another person, help them to understand their problem, listen to them, reflect back, guide them to understand what is going on. Share your experience, and let them figure out what they want to do. This is deep and lasting help, what the best mentors do. Giving advice rarely is helpful unless specifically contracted for. For example: "I have some experience in shopping for a loan. Would you like to hear about what I've tried?"

3. THE AVOIDER

The avoider may be a good listener, but she shares little of herself, often staying stuck in endless small talk that even she feels bored with. There are many reasons for "avoiding" deeper contact, but most of them center on fear of some kind. Fear of sounding foolish, fear of not understanding, fear of not being understood, fear of boring others, or simply (my own personal demon), an existential self-doubt.

We vary greatly in how much we choose to reveal of ourselves in conversation. That's up to you. There are times to trust and show your vulnerabilities, and times when it's best not to. But Mindful Conversation means "talking about what matters to you." If you are unwilling to dare to talk about what matters to you, then you will remain an outsider. The door is open. Walk through it when you're ready.

If you see yourself as an Avoider, then it's time to think about what could make it easier for you to open up. What are you afraid of? If you revealed a bit more of yourself, what is the best that might happen? What is the worst? What do you think would probably happen? What are you gaining by hiding? What are you losing?

One approach to inching out of the shadows is to make a list of 3 - 5 topics of conversation (include yourself, but also stretch beyond just yourself) that you would genuinely like to talk about. Practice ways to introduce these topics. Commit to yourself to introduce at least one of them in a conversation this week. Start with someone whom you feel more comfortable with. It doesn't have to be a long conversation. Give it a try.

4. THE INTERRUPTER

We all interrupt others at times. This pattern shows up a lot, particularly in couples who have been together for some time. As soon as one starts talking, the other subconsciously thinks, *Oh, I know where this is going. I don't need to listen anymore.* It's an easy trap to fall into, and it flies in the face of the core value of Respect.

As with many unconscious habits, the big challenge is in becoming aware of when you are interrupting. Overcoming this habit requires motivation and focus. You may well need an aide to help you. Consider telling someone that you're close to that you want to break this habit. Ask them to wave at you or indicate in some way when you interrupt. When you become aware and you're tempted, instead of interrupting, try repeating back to your CP what you think she said. If she acknowledges that you heard correctly, then it's your turn to talk, but if not, keep repeating back what you understand until you can get her to agree that you've "heard" her message. (This is a great listening exercise also.)

5. THE NON-LISTENER

Some people just don't know the meaning of the word "listen." They don't. Ever. Such people tend to be "Performers" (from the Conversation Style Guide, Chapter 3) on steroids.

Mindful Conversation, as I've said repeatedly in this book, is a balancing act between speaking and listening, with listening often being the more pivotal role. Listening is the single most neglected skill. Learning how and committing to being a good listener is perhaps the most effective step you can take to enhance your conversation and your relationships.

If you are seriously lacking in this department, it is hard to make the shift alone. If you're intent about changing, get some support. Find a book, a friend, or a teacher you trust. Invest in yourself.

6. THE WANDERER

The wanderer is like a leaf blowing in the wind, directionless and lost. One of the aims of this book is to help you to become intentional in your conversation.

Spontaneity is a hallmark of good conversation. But spontaneity within a framework of intentionality. Mindful Conversation means thinking seriously about who you want to be, what roles you want to play, and what tone you wish to adopt, in your conversation.

In any conversation you might talk as a friend, or as a subject matter expert, a parent, teacher, or student. Your tone could be warm and loving, or it could be curious, or perhaps deliberately skeptical. Set your intention first, then hold it close in your mind during the conversation.

The four values of the C.A.R.E. (Curiosity, Awareness, Respect, Empathy) model may help you set your intention. Within such a framework, you can play or be serious. You can speak or listen. You can be bold or cautious. Conversations often have complicated maps. Set an intention. Let it guide you to stay on track.

7. THE PUPPET

The puppet is frequently "triggered" by a strong emotion, that rises suddenly, seems to take over, and often prompts him to say something that causes lasting or deep harm. We all get triggered at some time, but the puppet seems particularly to be the victim of his emotions. This problem is discussed in more detail (Chapters 20 & 21). The sources of this behavior can go very deep and can hardly be overcome in a brief assessment. A good place to start is to become more aware of the people, topics and / or situations that trigger you. Make a list, or when you're next triggered, write down the circumstance. This increased awareness alone can begin to help you move forward. Begin now. It could save a marriage, a job, a family, a deal or a friendship.

YOUR SCORE

The fact that you're reading this book, took this quiz and scored yourself means that you're already on your way. The lower your score, the better. Assuming that you're honest and aware of your own habits, if you scored 7 or below, you're doing great.

Congratulations! Keep it up. 8 to 14 is average. You can get by, but there's room for improvement, if you want to be above average. If you scored above 14, it's time to get to work.

I hope you enjoyed and learned from taking the quiz. If you're looking for fresh topics for conversation, conduct your own survey. Ask your friends about their pet peeves of conversation. Initiate a conversation about conversation.

You're welcome to print and share this assessment quiz with anyone who might enjoy it. Please share it gently, compassionately, in the spirit of Mindful Conversation.

Notes from the Journey

Core Awareness: Small bad habits can become large barriers to mindful conversation.

Core Value: Respect – for the language. Many of these "sins" grow out of lazy, unconscious thought and word usage. Pay attention and commit yourself to improving your conversation habits.

Core Skill: Setting an intention, monitoring your progress, rewarding yourself when you succeed.

Core Tools: Attention, intention, retention.

Next Steps

This assessment is an awareness tool. Write, talk about, or reflect in whatever way you wish on any insights about yourself. Any surprises? Use this tool to help you clarify areas you'd like to work on.

Section 3
My Summary and Action Plan

1. My Points of Awareness / Insights:

2. My Potential Implementation Challenges:

3. My Action Plan:

Part IV

The Me - Me Conversation: Connect with Yourself

Chapter 18
Exploring the Me - Me Conversation

*"No, Dad. I don't object to talking with you,
it's just that I prefer talking to myself.*

Who is your most frequent intimate confidant?

    A. Your spouse / partner

    B. Another family member

    C. Your best friend (other than spouse / partner)

    D. Your pet

    E. Your therapist / minister / counselor

    F. None of the above

The correct answer for most of us is "none of the above." The person you talk to most frequently and intimately is the person you are around the most, yourself. Talking with yourself is what I call the "Me – Me" or the "Second Conversation." This is where we work out our feelings, obsess over doubts and anxieties, replay blunders, dream of fantasies, relive moments of pride and satisfaction, and muddle with existential despair. In conversations shared only with yourself, you rehearse and create stories about who you think you are and who you'd like to be.

The Me - Me Conversation is completely ignored in most approaches to conversation. Yet it is absolutely central to who we are and how we converse. Like that other sub-conscious sanity check, night dreams, we would barely survive without our "day dreams," this internal, self-talk. The Me - Me Conversation is our most intimate conversation. It reflects our search for a fundamental identity. It sets the rules and the tone for our external conversations.

Most people wouldn't even recognize this internal dialogue as a conversation. But it is. It consumes a huge amount of mental and emotional energy. It dramatically influences how you listen (or don't), how you talk (or don't), and frequently, how you succeed or flounder.

What is this voice that talks to you when no one else is listening? Who is this boss that lives inside your brain? And what does he / she want?

The internal conversation is you creating your "story," how you define yourself, who, in your own mind, you are. You become who you tell yourself you are. The Me - Me conversation is the loudest, most important conversation of all.

Luck is with you on this one. The Me - Me Conversation is the only conversation where you hold all the cards. No one else even knows (or cares) what your internal "boss" says to you. Only you care. Or you should.

As I've said before, you wrote this story so you can change it. When you change your story, you change your life. This is not to say that changing your story is easy. It is not. It takes courage, patience and extended, focused work. But you can do it.

The Power of Me - Me Talk

Amanda is going to a party. She parks her car on the street. As she buttons up her coat and walks the block and a half to the party, she is deep in conversation (with herself). *"I don't like parties. I should have stayed home. Who will I talk to? What will I talk about? I don't have anything to say. I should have worn my blue dress instead of these stupid grey pants. They make me look fat. I felt so left out at the party I went to last weekend. I'm late again. Everyone will already be there. I'll be alone, no one to talk to. These people are idiots anyway. I don't even want to talk to them. I'll quickly get a drink. That's what I'll do. I'll head for the bar as soon as I get inside."*

Of course, anything could happen at the party. Amanda can't control that, but she is carrying a story about the person she will be at the party. Her story is unrelentingly negative. Her self-talk is a catalogue of negative beliefs, thoughts, feelings and assumptions that swirl about inside her mind. Her story stacks the deck against her and reinforces her belief that she has little to offer, looks bad, is an unlovable loser randomly dropped into a crowd of idiots. Her negative Me - Me conversation is a one-way street that dead-ends in anxiety, stress, isolation and depression.

Negative self-talk undermines the best in us, exaggerating and distorting problems until they seem like the full landscape of life. Amanda first creates failure in her mind, then she finds it in the world. Her relentless negative self-talk is the single biggest barrier to her leading anything close to a fulfilling life. It is what some Buddhists refer to as "the second arrow." It is the deep source of her suffering. It puts any hopes for her happiness, good decision making, and lasting, full relationships out of reach.

Our stories have only the power we give them. We fall in love with, and are seduced by our own fiction.

We all carry stories within, mostly unconscious, adopted from parents, teachers, movies, songs, friends, past traumas, dreams that never came true, and advertisements depicting how we should look and be. The problem is not that we engage in Me - Me conversation. Our brains have been at it for millennia. Even when we outgrow our stories, they stay with us, like an old shirt, too short in the sleeves and worn at the collar. We can't - and shouldn't - stop the self-talk. We can, and *must,* turn this story, our biggest adversary, into our closest ally.

It's not the events outside - who's at the party or what she's wearing or what happened at last week's party - that shape Amanda's experience. Rather it is her thoughts and her interpretation, the meaning she gives these events, the story she tells herself about what is happening. What happens "outside" can give us temporary pleasure or pain. What happens "inside" is the source of our enduring suffering ... or joy. Amanda's "story" is not *the* truth. But it is *her* truth, and as such, it defines how she feels, how she speaks, and how she behaves.

Change your story and you change your life. A certain amount of grief and disappointment is unavoidable. Loss is part of life. But suffering is optional. We bring the suffering on ourselves.

Amanda has work to do. And a party to attend.

Amanda at the Party

Let's follow Amanda at the party and see how she does. She heads for the bar, grabs a drink, then off to the food table. But she is already full – filled with the story she told herself just before entering the house. Frank, whom she doesn't know, approaches from across the room.

> Frank: (Smiling) "Did you try this cheese?"
>
> Amanda: "No."
>
> Frank: (Offering her a piece) "It's delicious. You should try it."
>
> Amanda: "I don't like strong cheese." (She looks down.)
>
> Frank: "Well, I promised my friends I'd bring them some." (He fills plate and departs.)
>
> Amanda: Downs her drink and waits briefly, hoping that someone else will appear. Soon, she leaves the party, "Idiots," she says to herself. "All idiots."

Amanda and Frank's conversation was short, barely even a conversation, but it contains important, revealing words and actions. We'll return to Amanda and Frank in a bit. But first:

NEGATIVITY BIAS

Amanda is a victim of negativity bias, the habit of creating her story from negative ideas and then to dwell on the negative while rejecting the positive. Most of us notice and respond more strongly to negative news and feedback than to positive. The brain works to keep us safe. Even if there are no outer threats, these negative stories we tell ourselves quickly become the lens through which we view our world. They create our identity, and it is not a pretty (or an accurate) picture.

Your stories become the themes for your Me - Me conversation. The resulting negativity bias impacts relationships, identity, finance, decision making, political opinions, first impressions, responses to movies, books and people – in short, your life.

We're not heading for Positive Thinking 101 or "get over it" advice. This is not about smiling your way to happiness. It is about reclaiming the whole you – prouds and sorries, challenges and triumphs. It is about recognizing your true feelings and using them to guide you ever closer to expressing the full, authentic you. It is about raising awareness of the positive, while not neglecting real threats or negative stimuli. It is about making your mind your #1 supporter, not your chief adversary.

AMANDA SHIFTS HER INNER CONVERSATION

Now imagine that Amanda is approaching the same party. Her self-talk goes like this: "I wonder who I will meet at this party. I don't know anyone, so anything is possible. I'm going to try to meet at least one person who really interests me. I feel nervous. I'm often uncomfortable at parties. I know it may take me a while to get into a conversation, but I have a lot to offer. I'd like to talk about the movie I just saw and the trip I'm planning. I'll stay patient and look for an opportunity. I'll relax, and let it happen."

Amanda's self-talk here employs the principles of Mindful Conversation. She is curious. "I wonder who I will meet." She is authentic. "I feel nervous. I'm often uncomfortable at parties." She is respectful and empathic towards herself. "I know it may take me a while to get into a conversation, but I have a lot to offer." She is prepared. "I'd like to talk about ..."

This is a different Amanda, now taking concrete steps to change her story. Her mindful self-talk doesn't guarantee that a Prince / Princess Charming will greet her at the door, but her chances for a good time, good connections and useful learning are vastly increased.

The Left Hand Column

The "left hand column" is a tool to help us look at our internal chatter and become aware of its impact on our inner conversation. Using this tool in combination with mindful reflection is an effective way to understand and begin to change your Me - Me conversation. The left hand column exercise grew out of research by Chris Argyris and Donald Schön and was further explored by Peter Senge, in *The Fifth Discipline*.

Let's reexamine Frank and Amanda's brief exchange, looking at Amanda's self-talk, and finally looking at how Mindful Awareness and Reflection could have created a very different kind of exchange.

The Left Hand Column exercise invites you to recreate a conversation (usually one that did not go well, or did not produce the results you hoped for) as accurately as possible. Then, in an additional (left hand) column, write your unexpressed thoughts and feelings. I have added the prompt to include non-verbal "talk" on the worksheet and a series of reflective questions to use after you've completed the worksheet. These questions are based on the principles of Mindful Conversation and are key to converting the insights from the Left Hand Column exercise into healing action.

If Amanda completed the left hand column worksheet, it might look something like this:

My Unspoken thoughts, feelings and behaviors	The Spoken Conversation
Hmm. He's cute. I wonder if we might connect somehow.	Frank: Did you try this cheese?
He's too cute. He'd never be attracted to me.	Amanda: No
He must feel obligated to say something.	Frank: It's delicious. Try it.
What a dumb thing to say. I've never even tried that cheese.	Amanda: I don't like strong cheese.
Now, what's he trying to prove. I can get my own cheese.	Frank: It's not so strong. Why don't you try a piece. Here.
	Amanda: No thanks.
I knew it. He's here with friends. Like everyone but me. Why do I even come to these stupid parties. I'm going home.	Frank: Well, I promised my friends, I'd bring them more cheese.
	Frank departs.

The very act of writing this dialogue and paying attention to her inner conversation will expand Amanda's awareness of how this self-talk distorts and undermines her experience. This new awareness shines a light on what is often referred to as "confirmation bias," the universal tendency to seek, recall, interpret or favor information that confirms what we already believe about a situation. Amanda's confirmation biases lock her into a self-defeating, self-built prison. She must expand her awareness before she can change either her inner or her outer conversation.

The Left Hand Column is a meta tool for uncovering the power of the unconscious. Moving beyond our own, distorted thinking requires a journey through honest self-reflection and discovery. The path leads through three moves, Awareness, Creativity, and Expression (that won't always proceed neatly and in order). We'll explore them in the remaining chapters of part IV of this book. If you want to study in more depth the power of "Internal Chatter," then I highly recommend Ethan Kross' excellent, *Chatter, The Voice in our Head, Why It Matters, and How to Harness It.*[21]

Your APR

A major shift is necessary to free ourselves from the type of negative belief and image that Amanda (and so many others) carry around inside our heads. Required is a process that you can employ over and over, in tough times and good, until your old patterns of thought are replaced by a new way of thinking, feeling and being. The process I recommend is called "APR." It has nothing to do with the finance term, Annual Percentage Rate, but perhaps these familiar letters will make it easier to remember.

In this process, the letters APR stand for:

Aware
Pause
Reflect

APR, for me, has been the key to the most significant, life-affirming, internal change that I have made in my adult life. I have used it for years and use it still. I use APR frequently when I coach others. I've seen it work miracles for many people who suffer, like Amanda, from stories that rob them of the opportunities they so desperately long for. APR is not an instant cure. It requires intention, patience, courage and practice.

In this chapter, I want to explore the first step, Awareness. I'll discuss Pause and Reflect in Chapter 19.

1. AWARE

We've talked a lot about awareness in this book already. Awareness is the starting point for all things Mindful. The root of mindfulness is to bring the full life experience into clear view. Awareness means acceptance. It means being able to see and feel our full range of emotion, to name the feelings, and to accept them for what they are, part of our life experience, comfortable or not. You cannot change what you cannot see. It all begins with awareness.

Some emotions are uncomfortable: anxiety, fear, shame, to name a few. You would probably prefer not to feel such feelings. Many people deal with discomfort by trying to cover it over, *without awareness*. Addiction is the best-known of such cover-up strategies. Whether it's addiction to drugs, alcohol, sex, gambling or more seemingly benign addictions such as technology, food, adrenaline rushes or binge TV, the key point is that you are working very hard to avoid feeling your feelings The thoroughly documented truth is that if you cannot see and name your feelings, you become their victim.

Brené Brown writes of the distinction between guilt and shame: Guilt = I made a mistake. Shame = I am a mistake. If you think you are a mistake, then every act of cover-up locks you tighter inside your self-made prison. The way out is straight through the door of awareness.

Emotion is one of the best sources of healing in life. But if you are not aware of your feelings, they will steal the life out of you. The choice is yours. Will your feelings be healers or stealers?

Unacknowledged and unexpressed feelings prompt you to unconscious actions often harmful to yourself or others. This is not to say that you should express every thought or feeling. The point is to be aware and then to make conscious choices about if, when, to whom and how to express what it is that you're hiding.

Looking at this reflective lens, Amanda might notice, "I thought he was cute. I felt attracted to him, but I immediately repressed this feeling and turned away. I would not have told him he was cute, never! But I could have smiled or shown some favorable response. Instead, I acted to protect myself from rejection ... before he could reject me."

Awareness includes examining your thoughts as well as your feelings: becoming aware of thought practices such as **filtering** (focusing only on the negative aspects of your experience); **catastrophizing** (exaggerating, seeing disaster at every turn); **blaming** (holding others responsible for your own problems or pain); **black and white thinking** (it's all or nothing, no shades of gray) and **over-generalizing** (drawing conclusions based on little or scant evidence).

Looking through this lens, Amanda might reflect, "One of my unconscious thoughts was, 'He'd never be interested in me.' Words like 'always' and 'never' are huge red flags for **black and white** thinking. Other than the fact that he paused briefly to talk and smiled at her, Amanda had no evidence that Frank was or was not interested in her. She assumed the negative and closed herself off to the experience.

Thanks to her curiosity, Amanda might now be aware, "I've always been sensitive. I remember how my mom so often told me, 'Don't wear your heart on your sleeve.' I turned that little phrase into 'Don't show your true feelings.' Unconsciously, I hid my attraction to Frank."

Common Myths

Once we have that initial awareness of how our negative self-talk is a way of hiding from ourselves, we are on the path of change. We can see how we resort to negative thinking when we feel alone, desperate, overwhelmed, convinced that we are bad, unworthy, too this or too that. Some of the most common self-talk stories are:

o The Victim - "Poor me. They're all out to get me."

o The Misunderstood - "I am complex and unique. No one understands me."

o The Unlovable - "I am too (_____ fill in the blank). No one will ever love me. I will always be alone."

o The Helper - "I am valuable only if am helping someone else. I must subjugate all my own desires."

o The Fraud - "I'm a fake. I must prove myself. They'll realize I don't know anything."

These imaginary stories beguile us with big lies: that we are fundamentally different from others, that we are not deserving of love or friendship; or that we are superior, the savior for mankind. Such stories are not true and not helpful. But they are highly seductive. They appear to absolve us of responsibility for our actions because the story is bigger than we are, too powerful to fight against.

Acknowledging that we have the power to change our story is a gigantic step to lasting personal change.

Questions for Reflection

The practices in the awareness phase are designed to shine a light on the unhealthy thoughts, feelings, images, and stories we adopt. To benefit from this new awareness, on the path to creating new, helpful images, it is essential to reflect on the self-image we carry around. Here are some reflective questions to ask:

o What is my self-image that I carry inside me? What impact does this particular image have on me? How does it show up in my life? (Be specific.) How does this self-image help or hinder me to be who I want to be?

o Is any part of this self-image true? What is the evidence for truth or falsehood? What parts are clearly false?

o What does this one dimensional image protect me from? What am I afraid of?

o What would happen if I changed or expanded this image?

o What new self-image can I show myself that is based on the truth as I now see it. What new image would reinforce the best parts of me, and motivate me to draw inspiration from who I want to be and would feel proud about.

Notes from the Journey

Core Awareness: We all tell ourselves stories about who we are and how we are doing. Our negativity and confirmation biases turn these stories into unconscious prison walls.

Core Value: Curiosity. Open to the truth of your own unconscious thoughts.

Core Skill: Reflecting on your own self-talk, being able to explore the stories you are telling yourself.

Core Tool: The Left Hand Column.

Next Steps

1. Set an intention, over the next week, to listen attentively to your self-talk.

2. In your journal, write a one or two sentence description of a story that you are telling yourself. Name the story (such as Victim Story, or Helper Story).

3. Now create a new, substitute story, one that rings true to you and that you find motivating. Give that story a name.

4. Practice incorporating the new story into your Me - Me conversation.

Chapter 19
"Conversational Calamity"

*"So, it feels like your amygdala has taken over.
What makes you say that?"*

Despite our best efforts, we all experience Conversational Calamities from time to time. By "Conversational Calamity" I mean what is often referred to as being "triggered," i.e. losing it; going bananas, coming unhinged, possessed, enraged, panicked, freaked out, blowing a gasket, going ballistic, flipping your lid ... etc. etc. So many phrases because this happens to all of us, too often, and it can be devastating.

I've been there, more often than I care to admit. I was triggered when first writing this chapter. Maybe even this exact part. Couldn't get it right. Almost threw it out. Almost threw out the whole book. Irrational despair.

Conversational Calamities: Marriages, careers, families, and friendships, carefully nurtured over years, are torn apart in seconds. Wars begin. Sometimes the damage is merely temporary. Sometimes permanent.

Conversational calamities are most effectively avoided or mitigated by careful attention to the last two steps in the APR process: **Pause** and **Reflect**.

Zack and Harriet

Zack and Harriet have two small children. Zack lost his job and is struggling. One evening, as Harriet gathers the day's scattering of toys and clothes, Zack puts on his parka, picks up his keys, and announces he's going out. "And leave me with this mess?" Harriet blurts. Zack's eyes narrow. In addition to everything, now his wife is talking to him in that same holier-than- thou voice of his mother. The voice he hates but hears so often inside his mind. "You were home all day while I was out pounding the pavement," he shouts. "It's your mess. You never pick up after the kids."

Harriet snarls back, "I get up at night to comfort the kids. I take care of them all day long. I clean the house and do the shopping. And what do you contribute, Mr. Bigshot?"

Zack stomps to the door. "We'll see how well you do without me around. I'm not listening to your crap anymore."

As the door slams behind him, Harriet yells, "Don't bother to come back. I'll be gone. With the kids."

The scene ends. An hour, a day or a week later, Zack returns. Harriet and Zack shove this conversation under the rug and co-exist again. Each nurses a feeling of betrayal. The next fight they have wraps itself around this one. The legacy is like a weight that they carry with them, dragging them down, killing the love, smothering the joy.

WHY?

In a calmer state, neither Zack nor Harriet would speak this way. In the moment, they both feel justified and respond in ways that seriously damage one another and their marriage. They are digging a grave for their marriage, one shovelful at a time. Their frustration and anger make it very difficult to short-circuit this negative spiral. To reverse and heal what is happening requires disciplined attention to the two final steps of the APR process: **Pause** and **Reflect**.

Daniel Goleman, in his book *Emotional Intelligence,* calls such calamitous conversations an "Emotional Hijack," and it is, in fact like being hijacked by your emotions. Calamitous conversations occur most frequently with the most important people to you: a domestic partner, a child, your boss , a parent, a work colleague.

Underneath the external conversation, Zack is telling himself a story that he would normally set aside, or at least modulate. He tells himself that Harriet is like his mother, whom he resents. He tells himself that Harriet is lazy, and that she is out to control him. In more rational moments, this story might occasionally show up but it would not take over his rational mind.

The Anatomy of a Calamitous Conversation

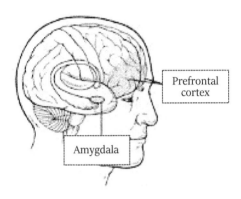

Triggering, many neuroscientists say, is directed from the amygdala, the most primitive part of the brain, trying, in the only way it knows how, to protect you. The thalamus, a small relay station responsible for receiving and transferring external sensations to the brain, forwards a signal to two very different parts of the brain: 1. To the prefrontal cortex (PFC, the executive or logical brain) and 2. To the amygdala, a small, almond shape collection of cells, from the primitive, limbic brain, a holdover from our reptilian ancestors.

The amygdala may be primitive, but it is no slouch. Until very recently, most neuroscientists thought that the amygdala operated pretty much alone as an "emotional czar." The most current brain science sees the brain operating as a network of networks, all dancing together, no single part operating independently. The amygdala operates in association with other parts of the brain,[24] but it processes information milliseconds faster than the prefrontal cortex, and it apparently acknowledges mostly the emotions we are likely to feel when threatened, such as fear and anger. You are cut off from your more normal, rational thoughts. Your thinking is limited to three possible responses: fight, flight or freeze.

The amygdala was once critical to survival, forever on guard for a surprise attack by a wooly mammoth. Most of such threats haven't existed for millions of years, but the amygdala never got the memo. Responding to the amygdala's alarm, the body goes into emergency survival mode: shallow breathing and hyperventilation, rapid heartbeat, oxygen deprivation to vital areas, dry mouth, cold and sweaty palms, trembling, obsessive thinking, blurry vision. You are triggered. A calamitous conversation is very likely to follow, with yourself or whomever you may be with. Your only real hope is to **Pause** and **Reflect**.

You desperately need your prefrontal cortex to participate in this decision. Best by far is to intervene, skillfully, *before* the amygdala and the limbic system take control. This is where the APR process comes to the rescue. We can simplify your response to being triggered into preventions (what you can potentially do *before* you are irrevocably triggered) and interventions (what you can do once you are clearly triggered and have made the decision to shift your fight freeze flight response).

Understanding Prevention

Awareness, as we have discussed, is the doorway to a more mindful approach. As a life practice and even before a potential triggering conversation starts, put yourself on alert for trigger events. Understand that we all get triggered from time to time. There is no need for shame. Through the Pause and Reflect phases of APR, you can start to shift triggering experiences from stealer to healer. In conversation (or whatever reflective medium you might choose) consider these questions:

1. Do you get triggered? Never, Rarely, Sometimes, Often.

2. What circumstances tend to trigger you? Review recent triggering events. Look for common circumstances.

3. Are there certain people who trigger you? Under what circumstances?

4. When you are triggered, do the circumstances remind you in any way of people or conditions from your past, especially from childhood? What associations tend to trigger you?

5. What is the cost (physical, emotional, financial ... to you? to others?) of past triggering events? How have incidents been disruptive, painful, stressful to you or others? How do you feel about yourself / others following such an event? How long does it take you to recover?

6. If you were someone else advising you on how you might better be aware of the circumstances that trigger you, how would you advise yourself to handle the situation?

Interventions

Even the best of preventions cannot always save you from being triggered. Interventions are about how to respond in such moments, to restore yourself to being your best self and to limit the damage.

The change begins when we shift from reactive mode into awareness and pause. Stop yourself. Take a breath. Tune into your feeling. Name the emotion and where in the body you feel it. For example: "I am feeling triggered. I am upset and angry.

I feel attacked. My heart is racing. My hands feel sweaty." Such a thought process begins to shift your center of being:

> *from* – past oriented, fear driven and blaming
> *to* – present oriented, open and understanding.

That's a monumental shift to your conversation. It won't happen overnight. You are unlikely to be successful every time. But over time, it can become your automatic, default style. APR can guide you. Is it time to start?

We'll explore four tools, all for use in the Pause and Reflect phases of APR. Consciously or unconsciously, you may well have used such approaches before, but now you are called to use them under emotionally charged, stressful conditions. The stakes are high. The pressure is on.

1. Intentional Stop

2. Emotional Distancing and Distracting

3. Language Shift

4. Ritual

Let's return, briefly, to the conversational calamity between Zack and Harriet. Zack's parting response was, "We'll see how well you do without me around. I'm not listening to your crap anymore." This is Amygdala speak: blaming, threatening, defensive. Zack is angry. He feels under attack. His response is a bomb that may cause serious, long-lasting damage.

1. INTENTIONAL STOP

We've explored the importance of taking a break when in conversation, creating space to set an intention, reconnect with your higher self, and pull back from the pressure of the moment. We looked at how a Mindful Pause can include moments of silence, a chance to breathe slowly and deeply, even a shift into play. Any of these can help steer you back on course. The difference, when you're triggered, is that now so much is on the line. Emotions are high. CP's are usually in no mood to back off. The wrong word, the wrong look, the wrong tone can take you down a one way path with little or no space for turn arounds.

Under such circumstances, you need to double down on the Mindful Pause. You are like the referee in a boxing match who comes between the contestants to call a stop in the action and give a fallen fighter a chance to stand back up. Only in this match-up, you are both referee and fallen fighter (triggered by emotion). It's time to pause the action before someone is permanently injured.

PAUSE. Cease all action and reaction. Take three deep breaths. Think only about your breathing. If possible, close your eyes, or at least look away from the center of the action. Perhaps you can even take a much longer breath: ten minutes, perhaps a day. Step away from the feeling. Step out of the action. Give your amygdala a break.

Of course, the last thing you feel like doing in such a moment is to pause and breathe. You more likely want to let 'em have it, charge in, all guns blazing. That is what Zack felt like doing, and that's what he did. Others, less inclined to attack, prefer to withdraw. But neither attack nor withdrawal works.

The Intentional **PAUSE** can become your go-to habit to help you grow into a more mature, productive mindful conversation partner. You will like yourself better. You will avoid the disasters of uncontrolled Conversational Calamities. You have a chance to work through trouble spots in your relationships, rather than resort to drugs, violence or your weapons and defenses of choice. Those around you will trust you and like being around you more.

The best and painless way to activate the Intentional Pause is to turn to that most essential bodily function, breathing. A deep conscious breath slows down the action and briefly halts the conversation. It fills your heart, lungs and brain with life-giving oxygen. When you take a breath break, you can either announce what you are doing. ("I need to take a break. Can we pause for a moment?") or you can do it without saying anything, without anyone else even being aware.

As long as you are alive, you have the power to breathe. As Tara Brach, author of *Radical Acceptance: Embracing Your Life With the Heart of a Buddha,*[25] writes, "Become still. Deepen your attention. Take a sacred pause ...When we pause, it gives us a chance to come home to our heart again."

So, breathe! Slowly, deliberately, deeply. Breathe, then count. Deep in, count slowly to four. Exhale while you count, again slowly, to four. If circumstances allow, do this three times. If you can't manage three, do two. If not two, then one. Nothing complicated. Just breathe and count. Create space for your brain to rest and your heart to reset.

Breathing is not the only way to create an Intentional Pause. Here are a few, easy additional approaches. Learn what works best for you and practice often.

o   If you have a regular meditation practice, call upon whatever style of contemplative work you do. A moment of recollection of your practice returns you to the sense of calm and peace that you feel in your practice.

o   Imagine a favorite place of beauty and peace, fix it in your mind's eye, and go there. The spot can be real or imagined: a favorite chair; a field; a beach – wherever you find peace and calm. Look around, take it in. Let peace infuse your body and mind.

- o Choose some part of the body, such as your feet or hands. Tighten the muscles as tight as you can. Then release. That's all. Don't race. Be deliberate about it. If time allows, you can work your way around the body. Start with toes, move to feet, ankles, calves and so forth.

- o Combine the tightening and releasing exercise above with a mantra such as, "With this action, I release and let go my anger (fear, resentment etc.). I am free." Repeat with each muscle tightening.

- o Use any repetitive prayer or mantra that soothes you. Decide on your word or phrase when you are relaxed. (It's too late once you are triggered.) Then repeat that word or phrase silently to yourself. Work to keep your mind focused on the sound you have chosen. Some people prefer affirmations, such as "I am calm and relaxed" while others prefer a known prayer, a short poem, an image, a chant or sound of any kind.

2. DISTANCING AND DISTRACTING

We all have feelings. Feelings make us come alive. They give us energy, motivation, and joy. They free us to explore and discover. They connect us to one another, through the power of empathy. Without feelings, life is a dull grey monotone. Feelings are our friends, much of the time, but they can also be our downfall.

For a vivid picture of both the healing and the stealing power of feelings, observe very young children. In one moment they are the image of love: sweet, pure, the essence of goodness and grace. But a moment later, if something goes awry, they can be consumed by a temper tantrum. They have *become* the feeling. Nothing else matters. Nothing else even exists. They experience the moment like a helpless victim, and in a way, they are because they have not yet learned the strategy or tools to distance themselves from the wave of emotion that overtakes them.

When we are triggered, locked into a Conversational Calamity, we become like a young child. We *feel like* we are the helpless victim. But a major difference between the mindful adult and the child is that the mindful adult has the experience and the wisdom to create distance from the feelings that imprison. We *have* feelings but we are not our feelings. Our job is to feel the feelings, let the heart steer us, and then to create distance between ourselves and our feelings when necessary, let the mind guide us to practical, appropriate actions. In other words, pause and reflect.

"Distancing" refers to any strategy that helps remove you from the feeling side of the equation, enabling you to engage the thinker within. Reflection strategies include ways for focusing more on the big picture, i.e. expanding your frame of reference beyond your own immediate concerns; distracting yourself from the emotionally stressful challenge; or even simply talking to yourself in the 3rd person. In your Me - Me conversation, avoid the word "I." Instead, use your name or the 3rd-person pronouns such as "he, she, or they." Such a linguistic trick helps you to create distance between your full Self and the self that is absorbed by the feeling of the moment.

For example, Zack says, "I am so tired. I do all the work around here. I come home, needing a little peace and quiet and what do I find?" All this "I talk" tends to reinforce his feelings. Instead of this language, he might say, "Zack is so tired. He does all the work. He comes home, needing peace and quiet and what does he find?"

Experiment to discover which of the above approaches fits for you. If you can actually take a longer break, I have found the distraction strategy particularly effective. My distractions of choice are taking a warm shower to "wash away" the dominating emotion, and taking a walk in nature to focus on life outside my immediate concern.

3. SHIFTING LANGUAGE

How can Zack acknowledge his strong feelings but express them differently? The specific language that we use impacts both how the speaker and the receiver feel. Zack's parting salvo was, "We'll see how well you do without me around. I'm not listening to your crap anymore." He gets his feelings out by delivering a bombshell threat that will outlive his feelings of the moment and poison his relationship with Harriet, potentially forever.

Here's another way, Zack could express himself: "I'm so frustrated and angry. It's a hard time for me. And I'm discouraged. I want to share the family and financial responsibilities equally. It's just so hard." The tone and impact are totally different. He is more open and vulnerable, no threats or blaming. He uses a present oriented, values statement rather than past oriented judgment. Zack is upset. He expresses his frustration clearly, but with very different language and a radically different impact.

With this new language, Zack exemplifies the values of Mindful Conversation – curiosity, authenticity, respect and awareness. He has taken a major step forward, requiring patience and courage. Not easy, but possible when you take time to PAUSE and REFLECT.

Here are several specific reflection tools to help you in this vital but difficult task of shifting your language:

o   Remind yourself that you are more than your feelings. When triggered, whisper silently to yourself, "I feel X, but I am not my X." Or try, "Zach feels angry, but he is not his anger." Repeat. "Zach feels angry, but he is not his anger." Breathe deeply between each repetition, take in what you are saying. Focus on the phrase.

o Speak empathically to your CP. When you are triggered, this can be difficult but not impossible if you have done your homework and become comfortable with responding reflectively *when you are not triggered.* Suppose Harriet had said to Zack, "I understand it's a difficult time for you. It hurts me too to see how discouraged you are. Let's explore how we can divide our roles, so you can pursue your job search and I don't feel so wiped out at the end of the day." Expressing empathy for another, automatically removes us somewhat from our own, all-encompassing feeling. Empathy is healing, both to sender and receiver.

o Avoid Inflated Language and Behavior. Zack, in his conversation with Harriet, says, "I'm not listening to your crap anymore." Referring to his wife's language as "crap" is highly inflationary, bound to intensify the angry feelings already dominating the scene.

Inflationary language includes "catastrophizing" or "over-generalizing." Typical examples are unconscious phrases like: "It's hopeless ... I can't possibly fix this ... the relationship is over ... we'll never get out of debt ... you don't care at all." This kind of exaggerated, catastrophizing thought and language is a one-way ticket to alienation.

A more effective thought pattern is to look at the evidence and restrict your language to the emphatically expressed, observable facts, e.g., "I have tried several times to fix this, but so far not been successful. This is hard for me."

4. RITUAL

Rituals are time-honored routines that create meaning in the mind of the beholder, and can serve to distance one from the stressful feeling of the moment. Rituals may be culturally inspired, such as religious services, prayers, even shaking hands; or they may be individually created, such as a particular way to organize your desk, or clothes.

Rituals have the ability to distract our attention away from our particular concerns, and on to the specific behaviors of the ritual, as well as to values and connections that are important to us.

Adopt or create rituals that you can use when you sense yourself being triggered. For example, the Mindful Pause (conscious breathing) described above can be fashioned into a ritual, if you practice it often enough and in a consistent manner. If that doesn't appeal, invent your own ritual, such as closing your eyes for a moment or folding your hands, any voluntary action that serves to remind you of the need to operate slowly and intentionally in this moment of potential crisis.

In summary, finding the best path out of a triggered situation is one of the most challenging, and potentially growthful, steps you can take toward more mindful conversation. We all are triggered from time to time, and the damage that can happen before we are even aware, can be so calamitous. If you practice these ways of pausing and reflecting, over time, you can shift your own patterns in a relationship or conversation. And changing how you show up has the greatest likelihood of changing how others relate to you. Such moves will create more mutually satisfying, more fulfilling, longer lasting and deeper relationships.

Personal Reflection

When I reflect on the APR process — as I often do — I feel that I am touching something almost sacred. Not that it is perfect or foolproof. It isn't. But when my wife Wendy and I have a breakdown, as we do, I turn instinctively to APR.

I may feel overwhelmed, even hopeless. I don't know what to say or do. APR becomes my mirror, my telescope and microscope. When I apply it diligently, I am almost always gifted with insights into my own fears and limitations. Sometimes I feel so alone and broken. But if I am true to the APR, I leave with a renewed sense of faith that I am on a life-giving path of growth and liberation. In the wonderful words of Osibisa, the Ghanian-British Afro-pop band's song, "We are going. Heaven knows where we are going. But I know we will get there."

I am going. And I know I will get there.

Notes from the Journey

Core Awareness: As with any problem conversation, the primary strategy for managing when you are in a Conversational Calamity (i.e. triggered) is to shift from a reactionary to a Mindful Conversation.

Core Value: Empathy, by definition, involves distancing. Connecting with someone else's experience and feelings (as opposed to solely your own) opens a new world.

Core Skill: APR: Aware. Pause. Reflect. When you are triggered, between the stimulus (the feeling) and the response (your words and actions) there is a moment of power, a moment when you have a choice. Seize this moment.

Core Tools: Intentional Pause, Emotional Distancing, Language Shift, Ritual. When triggered take a break. Go for a walk in nature, shift your language.

Next Steps

1. Take an inventory of when and under what circumstances you are most often triggered.

2. Evaluate how significant a problem this is for you. Is this an issue you can take on by yourself or should you find professional help?

3. If you decide to take it on yourself, go slow to go fast. Read this chapter slowly and carefully. Proceed with care and compassion for yourself.

Chapter 20
Reframe Your Story

*"I never could figure out my story, so I settled for
an empty frame."*

Deep down, we want to be known for who we are. But who
hasn't tried to look cool, or talk tough, or play coy, imagining
that this false image will work better than the real one? We
stash our vulnerabilities where we think no one will notice,
but sooner or later, we emerge from the trance, feeling
disconnected, disappointed and confused.

Authenticity

We sabotage our desire to be known mostly because of fear. Fear of vulnerability, of exposing our true feelings, of risking rejection and shame. We hide our true feeling even from ourselves. Is it better to bury your head in the sand or to see the storm on the horizon?

Of course, we all have things about ourselves that we're not so proud of. It's not that we must share all the dirty laundry. But when we are inauthentic, we are alone. When we model vulnerability, others often respond in kind. We connect in the magic of authentic connection. Stress, anxiety and isolation melt slowly, but melt they do when exposed to the light of day.

Our thoughts and feelings collectively constitute the story that we tell ourselves, as discussed in the last chapter. We have considerable control over these thoughts and feelings, but first we must become aware, i.e. conscious, of them. Awareness is power.

Basic Truths

A few vital truths, that we have already mentioned but bare repeating, have brought us to this point:

o We all have an external life (circumstances and events) and an internal life (what we tell ourselves about these external experiences). The chatter about internal life is what I've referred to already as "the story" we tell ourselves, or the Me - Me conversation.

o We invent and tell stories to make sense of our lives, to explain what happened and why, to find meaning in the otherwise seeming random events of our lives, to establish and confirm our identity.

o We have limited powers to influence the external circumstances of our lives. But we can learn to control our internal response to external events. This is where our real power lies. But it is often sleeping.

o Understanding and directing this internal interpretation means taking charge of the Me - Me Conversation. I've said it before, but it bears repeating. A certain amount of pain and loss are unavoidable in life. Suffering is optional. The suffering is embedded in the Me - Me conversation, in the (internal) story, not in the (external) events.

o One of the most powerful means of growth available to you is to change your internal conversation. Learn to talk to yourself with the same C.A.R.E. (Curiosity, Awareness, Respect, and Empathy) that Mindful Conversation teaches us to use in the Me - You Conversation.

Our internal story emerges from the shadows of our lives and our conditioning. We don't consciously decide what story we are going to tell ourselves about ourselves. When we take the trouble to examine our internal stories, we often learn that we are performing in someone else's production, playing a role that we have been assigned by the "boss" (aka, the Director, our defensive ego). The play and the character seem at first to be a given. They are not. Choosing our story and our character could be the most important decision we never make.

As psychologist Dr. Lisa Feldman Barret,[22] author of *How Emotions Are Made: The Secret Life of the Brain* puts it:

"Emotions aren't a reaction to the world; they actually construct the world." Most of us assume that the world is there, and we are placed (randomly?) in it. Actually, we create our world, day by day, thought by thought, story by story, in conversation after conversation. Because we create the story, we can also change it.

The Source

You cannot stop the internal chatter in your head. And nor in fact would you want to. As Dr. Ethan Kross puts it, this internal voice is what shapes your sense of identity, without which you are a leaf blown about in the wind.

Your choice is between listening to the *Voice of Fear* or to the *Voice of Hope*. The *Voice of Fear* (aka worry, despair, stress, tension, distress, depression, suffering, panic etc.). is ever knocking at the door. This is the voice of the ego. And the ego does not give up easily. This is the voice of your primitive limbic brain, that sees danger everywhere. On the other hand, the *Voice of Hope* is the call of your heart, the voice of your higher self, that sees the goodness in you and views your life as one of possibility. The Voice of Hope accepts that there are challenges, for sure. It sees the challenges as opportunities for growth, not woolly mammoths out to devour you.

Your job is to train your mind to nurture the Voice of Hope, and banish the Voice of Fear. Again, I don't mean to infer that this is easy. It is the most important goal of the Mindfulness part of Mindful Conversation. It is a lifelong process, but once you fully embrace it, you will start to reap the benefits. You are now the director of the script for your own life. Who will play the title role? Fear or Hope?

If you, the Director, have done a good job, then you are cast to be your best, most authentic self in a play that you like and believe in. Bravo. Express your gratitude to all the people and influences that created you, and to yourself for holding true. But if this director has a strong negativity bias, aka the Voice of Fear, the title role may be played by Mr. or Ms. Stupid, Ugly, Unlovable, Unworthy, Forever Poor, Victim, Outsider, Too Weird, Too Straight, Wrong gender, Wrong era, Wrong family, Wrong religion, Wrong race, Wrong country of origin, Too Short, Too Tall, Too This, Too That. So many stories to choose from. None of them true. But all of them ready to undermine who you really are and can be.

You either accept this director's decision and stagger through life, miscast in a role you never wanted in a play you don't like ... or you re-create your story, one Me - Me conversation at a time. Your conversations are your direct hotline to the director. You choose the role; you choose the story.

Your brain will try to convince you that the old story will protect you from pain. Your brain wrote that story. Your heart can change it. We free ourselves from the story by daring to speak authentically, first to ourselves and then to the world. This is the task. This is the path of Mindful Conversation.

A Story of Change

This is a true story of how a wounded, fearful woman overcame years of trauma and negative self-talk through a creative, daring act of imagination. The story is disturbing. I cite it here because it illustrates the power of courage, patience and will to replace long standing negative patterns of inner conversation with a new story. And it illustrates how a strong heart overcame a deeply conditioned brain and body.

Eve Ensler was 5 years old when her father began a practice of sexual abuse that continued until she was 10, at which time he pivoted to physical and emotional abuse. The father died 31 years later, without ever having apologized or made any amends, leaving his daughter overflowing with anxiety, shame and resentment.

Trapped in her story, Eve turned to writing and found herself working through details of her trauma, creating an apology written *in the voice of her father*. Important to note here is that the apology never happened in fact. Ensler created this new story solely in her mind.

Turning her imagination to the task of healing, Ensler was able literally to recreate her story, reshape her self-talk, in essence, to be born again. Reflecting back on her process of liberation, Ensler says, "The imagination is more powerful and persuasive than anything we can do. This is the most liberating thing I've ever done. I'm [now] living in my story ... [the false story] is over. It's done." For further details, you can find Eve Ensler's story in her book, *The Apology*.[23]

Most of us will not have to go to the extreme that Eve Ensler did. The point is that she did, and you can, change your limiting thoughts and story. Change your story, change your life.

Moving to Action

Shifting your self-talk is not easy, but it is doable. The basic process again is APR: Awareness, Pause, Re-think.

It also can't be done without a lot of love, self-love. As Brené Brown writes in her book *Imperfect,* "Owning our story and loving ourselves through the process is the most radical thing we can do."

It all starts with awareness, followed by the pause, stopping the automatic chatter and creating the intention to shift a revised story. The new story has been fertilized by your new awareness, but it is young and tender and vulnerable. You must nurture this embryo and bring it to term. This is your work.

The day arrives when you can no longer hold back. The new story is ready to be born. Conversation is the most readily available means. Bring this new story into your conversation. It can be explicit, or implicitly the context for how you talk, what you say, how you listen.

Conversation is not the only medium. How you express this new story is totally up to you. Eve Ensler wrote a book of fiction, based on her true life experience. It worked wonders for her. I wrote a memoir that had the same basic intent and result. Your way could be similar, or very different. You may wish to start off very privately. Totally fine. But in my experience, the process is not over until you have gone public in whatever fashion works for you.

You'll need an activity or medium that allows for deep reflection and expression. It could be solo walks in nature or soaking in hot baths. It could include meditation. Individual therapy or joining a support group can be enormously helpful. I often coach people through the process. Maybe the public expression for your new story is with your family. Or a special relationship. Those who gravitate to the creative arts often turn to painting, composing or playing music, writing a memoir, poetry, fiction. Maybe gardening or cooking or bicycle riding creates the space for your imagination to do this work. Or combinations of the above. This is a healing journey. There is no one right way. Whatever ways you choose, remember that the purpose of your journey is to clean away those parts of your story that don't serve you so you can create a new story that resonates with the image of a refreshed, rejuvenated you.

Speaking from experience, let me say that if your journey is anything like mine, it will be the best trip of your life. Give this new you what he / she needs, and you have a friend for life. That friend is you.

Eve Ensler did it. You can too.

My Story of Reinvention

For much of my life, I suffered from a condition I'd never even heard of, Imposter Syndrome. No matter what successes I had, I doubted my future ability to meet new circumstances, certain that everyone around would soon realize that I was a fraud. My inner life was a sea of doubt. A new challenge sent me into a pit of despair. At work, I was certain that I would soon be discovered and revealed as the incompetent charlatan that I knew I was.

Imposter Syndrome, I later learned, is a well-known psychological condition that affects many people, without regard for talent, intelligence or achievement. The inner story has nothing to do with the external reality. It is the inner story that matters! I beat myself up and forgave myself, over and over.

I certainly never said to myself, "I am in the midst of APR," but I found myself there. Consciously and subliminally, I began to rewrite my story. Bit by bit, I changed my story from, "I can't possibly do this" to "Yes, I can."

Step 3, Re-think, was a hit and miss proposition. I recognized that I couldn't keep this major life challenge inside. I had to proclaim it out loud, in as many ways as I could and to as many people as would listen. I had to risk exposing the authentic me first to myself, but then to the world. I had to embrace, forgive and celebrate my own vulnerability. Eventually I wrote what became a multiple award-winning memoir about this experience (*King of Doubt*), three years of intense work, but it changed my life. I was no longer alone and shamed by my challenge. The telling made me stronger within and became an avenue to deeper connection with friends, colleagues, and many readers whom I never even met.

The New Story

Your new story is based no longer where the brain sees fear, but where the heart finds hope.

When you learn to love yourself, you will love the world around you. When you love the world around you, it will love you back.

Notes from the Journey

Core Awareness: We write our own stories. They have only the power that we give them.

Core Value: Curiosity. Examine your story.

Core Skill: Learning to change your story

Core Tool: Breaking a story down into small parts that you then work to change.

Next Steps

1. Think about an event from your past that you interpreted in a negative or limiting way. Describe the story that you told yourself that led you to that interpretation. Invent a new story, that you could have told yourself, that could have led you to a different meaning.

2. What is THE BIG STORY that you tell yourself now? If it has elements that limit you, play around with it. Aware that this is not an overnight process, commit to creating an alternative story that feels plausible to you. Use this story to shift the negative tone of your Me - Me Conversation.

Part 5

The Universal Conversation: Connect with Life

Chapter 21
The Universal Song

*"I'm searching for our Universal Song.
Any idea where we put it?"*

Up to now, this book has focused on exploring conversation in two arenas: the interpersonal (Me - You) and the intra-personal (Me - Me). There is a third arena, the meta- personal. More abstract, a little harder for some to wrap their head around, but equally important. This is about our oneness, our common humanity, the conversation and the relationship we have, or fail to have, with the life force beyond our own immediate circle.

Some call this territory "God." Others call it "Mother

Nature". Or the "Tao". "Ubuntu" is the Zulu word. Many names for a universal concept. I like to call it the "Universal Song" because it reflects our common voice, be it Christian, Buddhist, Moslem, Hindu, the ancient gods, or future myths that will find their way into our consciousness.

If none of the words mentioned above work for you, think of it as a consciousness that stretches out beyond you or me, beyond time and space. Use whatever name works for you. What is important is to meet this Underlying Reality (as author Mark Nepo[27] refers to it) head on. This is the 3rd level conversation, the Me - Us connection.

Connection in this arena is a topic in many metaphysical books. I'll address the Me - Us conversation here in relationship to our larger conversation: how we look at one another; what we trust; where we place our faith; how we relate to the Earth; what we see as the meaning and purpose of life. This connection shapes our daily, personal interactions, the stories we tell, and who we ultimately are, beyond birth and death, before we get up in the morning and after we go to sleep at night. This conversation, engaged in millions of times every day in millions of ways, shapes our society, our government, the values we espouse, whom we choose for leaders and why we follow those whom we follow. When we engage in this 3rd conversation, we are often quite alone and never more united. We are one with the life force, whatever we call it, even, if we don't believe there is any such thing.

The Universal Song

I was first introduced to the concept of "Universal Song" by Michael Stillwater, in his award-winning film, *The Search for the Great Song*. The film asserts, and demonstrates, that there is an "inner song" built into our souls, that connects all experience, beyond language, beyond national, ethnic or religious culture. The sound is universal, one that all of us, maybe even all animals, maybe even all plants, can "hear". We hear this sound, more with the heart than the ears. There is a whisper of hope, curiosity, and creativity in every note. This is the harmony of the universe, singing to itself.

Personally, I embrace this concept of the "Great Song." Mindful Conversation exists with or without words. This is the higher purpose of conversation, to connect us with the core of our being – our oneness, our kindness, our place in the universe of being, our sense of belonging and meaning.

In the United States, as I write, many observe that we are in an epidemic of loneliness, depression, polarization and addiction. Why? Could it be that we have lost touch with this "Life Force"? On some level, we have become obsessed with the self and out of touch with the self-less. Preoccupied with the material world, out of touch with the spiritual. We have lost sight of our North Star, become so alienated that we no longer recognize our common humanity. Trust seems to be at an all-time low, and conspiracy theories lurk around every corner. We are more polarized than at any time since the Civil War. A what's-in-it-for-me spirit of distrust and spite has crept into our national zeitgeist. Not everywhere or everyone, but this "other pandemic" is widespread, and deadly.

Our highest ideals and our democratic way of life are threatened. Our guiding light is obscured in the clouds. How can we improve on where we have fallen short and recover what has served us so well over so many years and such change?

One way, perhaps the only way, to hear our universal song is to start talking, listening and singing to one another differently. It helps greatly when our leaders model responsible dialogue. Without the modeling at the top, we will never create the kind of change I am talking about. But no matter who sits at the top, this change must be embraced in kitchens and kindergartens, schools and offices, bars and streets. In short, by you and me.

The me / me talk is at the heart of individual consciousness. We give meaning to our lives by creating our personal mythology, our stories. We cannot, and we should not, discard these stories. Another way, of course, of spreading a broader sense of meaning is through our me / you talk. This is how we learn about others and work out our daily co-existence. We learn how to relate to our "tribe." Most of us define our "tribe" narrowly, as family and friends, perhaps colleagues and customers. This relational group is frequently further restricted by an insistence on common language, ethnicity, gender, interests, religion, region, nationality, etc. Such identities are natural and useful. But they also become barriers to a "common humanity." They create a dualistic thinking: us and them.

Connecting with the Life Force

Some will immediately reject the concept of a common humanity or life force as too "woo woo." But many of us have, at least in moments, come to understand that there is something beyond the narrow ways we define what is meant by the word "me." When we accept the idea of a common humanity, we acknowledge the existence of something (by whatever name) that binds us, beyond what we can fully know. It is a mystical feeling and a sense of oneness, an inner knowing that we are not alone. We are one.

Some connect with this awareness through prayer or meditation. Others take a walk in nature. A mother may feel it while looking at her baby. A painter may sense this mystical connection while painting. A singer on the stage or in the shower. An athlete may know it when something beyond his own abilities takes over and he responds from someplace beyond himself. Some call it being "in the flow." Regardless of name, something beyond your ego, beyond your abilities, knowledge or identity is in there leading the way.

This "something" is frequently experienced in the most still and quiet of times: when you hear, really hear, the call of the wind or fully experience the wonder of a flower, or when you are engaged with something (or someone) that you love, so deeply that it takes you beyond your ego existence, into another realm of being. This experience is another aspect of life, my life, your life, our life, but encountered from a deeper place. Access to this realm draws on faith in something beyond yourself and then to let go and allow.

Connecting with this life force demonstrates that you and I, regardless of "tribe," share a common origin and a common destiny. Our differences are minor and transitory. Our oneness is fundamental and everlasting.

For me, this profound sense of oneness is always there. That is not to say that I am in touch with it all the time. But even when I am stressed or upset or overcome by a sense of urgency, I know, in the depth of my being, that this oneness is the truth of existence, always there, waiting for me to let go and open to it.

Connecting in this way is level 3 conversation. When we live from this truth, we become part of the glorious symphony of life. We were all born in the same way. We walk the same path, albeit in different shoes. Our lives travel from birth to death, along this one well-worn path of oneness.

A Vision of Harmony

I live near the top of a hill. When I leave that hill and head into town in the afternoon, I am frequently greeted by the most glorious sight, the sun painting the hills on the far side of the valley. The meadows and the ridge glow with pride. The warmth fills me, body, mind and spirit. No matter my mood or preoccupation of the moment, I am lifted to a higher realm. In such moments, I am myself, and I am more than myself. I am connected to the life force that came long before me and will be here long after I am gone. It is a feeling of pervasive peace, the fullness of life. This is a conversation I do not want to miss.

Millions who bow humbly at the altar of our common humanity have had similar experiences. The skills for connecting on level three are no different from the skills of connection that we've discussed throughout this book. The C.A.R.E. Model still serves as a foundation.

1. **Curiosity**. Buddhists talk about "beginner's mind." It's about questioning assumptions, asking naive questions, developing a tolerance for ambiguity, opening your being to what is possible. Let the great drama of life fill you, teach you, entertain you, and help you keep growing as long as you live. Always be curious.

2. Speak and listen with **Authenticity.** When I connect from my essence, the barriers disappear. My core is the same as hers and his and ours and theirs. Speak from this place. Let down the mask. Reveal the deeper essence of who you are. Connect with me, and when I let down my mask, we discover that we are one and the same.

3. **Respect**. We all compete. We get angry, frustrated and self-righteous. When we talk with respect, we more readily transcend such fleeting emotions, and acknowledge our common humanity. We all want

respect. This is universal and eternal. Let your words and your non-verbal messages communicate this bedrock identity.

4. **Empathy** is the core skill of relationship. Like the air we breathe, empathy infuses every step of Mindful Conversation. You will seek to know and understand me; I will seek to know and understand you. It isn't hard. We are, after all, one.

It Matters

I cannot presume to say more about why this connection with our common humanity should matter to you. But I can say why it is so vital to me.

When I am in touch with this oneness of life, I am more me, stronger, more loving, calmer, accepting, nonjudgmental, at peace. Though I may be physically alone, I am joined to millions. How can I be lonely? I have friends everywhere. How can I keep from singing?

I love the inner peace that fills me. I don't need to worry about my place, the impression I make, the recognition I may or may not receive. Stress falls away. I am home.

I am one with all time and all life, all suffering and all joy. I am one tiny grain of sand on the beach of life. And I am the beach.

I believe that our survival as a species depends on our learning and embracing this profound experience of connection and expression. And I believe also that the survival of our pluralistic democracy, this precious legacy that we have nurtured for almost 250 years, is equally beholden to our modeling and teaching anyone who will listen, how to engage in this wonderous, life-altering sense of oneness. No one person, no matter their position or power, can do it alone. This is a job for all of us. Together, we can.

Epilogue

I sat at my desk almost every day for close to four years, writing this book. When the manuscript was finished, I had a moment of doubt. Doubt is familiar territory for me, part of the journey — my journey anyway. I wrote a whole book (*King of Doubt*) about my struggles with self-doubt. The doubt I refer to at the conclusion of writing this book was short lived. It morphed into gratitude for the opportunity, and pride, that I had seized the moment, declared my stance, and followed my heart through to its logical destiny.

Articulating the topic of Mindful Conversation has fed my soul. Writing the book and practicing Mindful Conversation have made my life so much richer, my conversations more deeply satisfying, my relationships closer, my inner pieces more peaceful.

As a way of closing, I'd like to share some of what I've learned, relearned, or integrated deeper thanks to the writing process. This is a chance for me to savor the memory and to share my personal experience with you.

A story may help to illustrate. The region where I live, Ashland, Or. in the Rogue Valley, just north of the California border, was recently hit by devastating wildfires that scorched two adjacent towns and demolished over 2,300 dwelling units and countless businesses. Thousands became homeless within a few hours. Many people joined together to support those who had lost everything. I volunteered at a disaster relief supply center, distributing food, clothing and items that I had taken for granted for years. On my shift, an elderly woman shuffled in, supported on the arm of her middle-aged daughter.

"I'm so sorry for your loss," I said.

"Thank you for helping," she replied.

"You've been through a lot."

She nodded. "Yes, but we keep going. Thank you again."

She put some cans of soup, bread, cereal and a dozen eggs into her bag. We were done. We each turned to our next tasks. As she departed, something called to us both. Simultaneously, we turned. Our eyes locked, two souls separated by the River of Fortune. How easily our roles could have been reversed. She smiled, a smile that slipped directly into the core of my being. We had never met before. We were unlikely to ever meet again, but for one eternal moment, we were both lost to any sense of separateness, we were one. We connected, without words. Her smile lives on and gives me strength and inspiration, now many months later.

I would not trade that moment for anything. A sacred, silent moment of Level 3 conversation. Level 3 is beyond words.

Feelings always matter, whether they are spoken or not, even when we are not aware of them. We are fragile beings in a fragile world. My conversation falls short more often than I wish. Too often, I have been "triggered" by an over-zealous amygdala. It feels bad at the time, but it's also an opportunity for insight and growth. The key is to pause, notice and reflect. Mistakes are the best teachers, and I enjoy learning.

Two steps forward and one sideways. Every step contains forward momentum, as long as I remain open, aware and accepting. I vow never to let my heart harden around mistakes. Go for growth. My growth is our growth. When I am true to me, I am a beacon of light for a "kinder, gentler" world. I need only stay curious, bold and humble.

Mindful Conversation has helped me discover new friends. Mostly I am referring to people whom I have known for some while, but not fully appreciated. When I listen deeply and curtail my judgments, I come to understand and then, almost invariably, to like and appreciate them more. It's like opening an envelope, expecting to find a bill but finding a check instead.

There is one friend in particular, someone I've known for a long time, but too often felt judgmental towards. Mindful Conversation has profoundly affected how I see him, finally with more compassion and understanding. I dare call it love. I've known this guy all my life. What a difference it makes to feel this way about myself.

This book, as you are aware if you made it this far, is about a philosophy of relating. The need to connect and express has defined our species since the days of the woolly mammoth. It is not hyperbole to say that our survival depends on finding and promulgating solutions to this need. Some will relate to Mindful Conversation; others, of course, will not. You've stuck with me this far, so I think we're in it together. Thank you for the pleasure of your company.

To embrace these concepts, I find I must be both humble, and proud.

Humility allows me to surrender to the "magic" that is deep human connection. Surrender requires faith, and faith requires humility. I also need pride. Pride in who I am, who I can be, and who we collectively are. We are worth it. I am worth it.

I hope that the journey I've described in these pages does not overwhelm you. Three things, maybe that's all you need remember:

1. Show Up
2. Show You Care
3. Show Your True Self

I'll meet you on the path.

Peter Gibb

Ashland, Oregon, 2021

Smile

"The other dogs told me my bark was worse than my bite, but this book changes everything."

Additional Reading

Conversation is an evergreen topic. This book is neither the first nor the last on the topic. I have been a student of the subject for decades and owe a debt of gratitude to the many who have pondered deeply, struggled with, and written about this complex subject. Although the framework for Mindful Conversation is uniquely my creation, many of the specifics originated with others, too numerous to mention.

I'd like to acknowledge my students and coaching clients, who teach me constantly from the field, where theory gets tested in the hearts and minds of real people, engaged in real relationships, real conversations. You are my teachers and my reason for continuing to pursue this topic.

Among writers, I will mention here, just a few of the most prominent for me:

Carl Rogers, a giant in the history of humanistic psychology, opened my eyes and my heart and brought me joyously out of the dark ages. I site particularly his groundbreaking, *On Becoming a Person,* Houghton Mifflin, 1961. I was so fortunate to have the life changing experience of spending two weeks with Carl at a workshop in 1974.

Jack Kornfield got me hooked on Mindfulness in books such as *After the Ecstasy, the Laundry*, Bantam Books, 2000. More recently, I have followed the inspiring, heartfelt words of Tara Brach, *Radical Acceptance,* Bantam Dell, 2003, and her delightful podcasts.

On the subject of Communications, there are many, excellent books on the subject, and quite a few not so good ones. Doug Stone and Sheila Heen's *Difficult Conversations,* Penguin Books, 2010, ranks right at the top. I also benefited greatly from Will Wise's *Ask Powerful Questions,* 2017, and enormously from Ethan Kross' *Chatter,* The Voice in Our Head, Why It Matters, and How to Harness It, Crown, Random House, 2021

From the recent psychological and cultural perspective, I have been particularly guided by Susan Cain's *Quiet,* Broadway Book, 2012; and Brené Brown's *Dare to Lead,* Random House, 2018. Mark Matusek's *Sex, Death and Enlightenment* has been around for a while, but as pivotal for me, as was Mark's teaching and encouragement.

There are so many others. Please refer to the bibliography for a more complete list.

Bibliography

Assaraf, John, *Innercise,* Waterside Press, Cardiff, Ca., 2018.

Barrett, Lisa Feldman PhD., *How Emotions Are Made: The Secret Life of the Brain*, Mariner Books, HarperCollins, 2018, New York, N.Y.

Barrett, Lisa Feldman PhD., *Seven and a Half Lessons About the Brain*, Mariner Books, 2021.

Berger, Warren, *A More Beautiful Question* and *The Book of Beautiful Questions,* Bloomsbury Publishing, New York.

Bonior, Andrea PhD, *Detox Your Thoughts,* 2020, Chronicle Prism, San Francisco, Ca.

Brach, Tara, *Radical Acceptance,* Bantam Dell, New York, N.Y. 2003,

Branch, Rhena and Wilson, Rob, *Cognitive Behavioral Therapy for Dummies,* John Wiley & Sons, New York, 2010.

Brooks, David, *The Second Mountain,* Penguin Random House, New York, N.Y., 2019.

Brown, Brené, *Daring Greatly, How the Courage to be Vulnerable Transforms the Way we Live, Love, Parent and Lead,* Avery, Penguin Random House, New York, N.Y., 2012.

Cain, Susan, *Quiet,* Broadway Books, New York, 2012.

Carnegie, Dale, *How to Win Friends and Influence People*, Simon & Schuster, New York, N.Y., 1936

Comstock, Craig K, *Enlarging Our Comfort Zone, A Life of Unexpected Destinations,* Willow Press, Ashland, OR.

Covey, Stephen R., The Seven Habits of Highly Effective People, Simon & Schuster, New York, 1990.

Edmondson, Amy C., *The Fearless Organization,* John Wiley & Sons, Hoboken, New Jersey, 2019.

Ensler, Eve, *The Apology,* Bloomsbury Books, New York, 2019.

Fine, Debra, *The Fine Art of Small Talk,* Hyperion Books, New York.

Fox, John, *Finding What You Didn't Lose,* Jeremy P. Tarcher / Putnam, New York, 1995.

Garner, Alan, *Conversationally Speaking, Tested New Ways to Increase Your Personal and Social Effectiveness,* McGraw-Hill, New York, 1997.

Gelinas, Mary, *Talk Matters,* 2016.

Gladwell, Malcom, *Talking to Strangers,* Little Brown and Company, Hachette Book Group, New York, 2019.

Goleman, Daniel, *Emotional Intelligence,* Bantam Books, New York, 1995.

Green, Barry, with Tim Gallwey, *The Inner Game of Music,* Doubleday, New York, 1986.

Hamlin, Sonya, *How to Talk so People Listen,* HarperCollins, New York, 2006. Hedges,

Hedges Kristi, *The Power of Presence,* Amacom

Isaacs, William, *Dialogue: The Art of Thinking Together,* Crown Business, 1999.

Kabat-Zinn, Jon, *Full Catastrophe Living, Using the Wisdom of Your Body and Mind to Face Stress, Pain and Illness.* Bantam, Doubleday, Dell, New York, N.Y. 1990.

Kenneally, Christine, *The First Word, The Search for the Origin of Language,* Viking Penguin, New York, N.Y., 2007.

Kross Ethan, Chatter: The Voice in Our Head, Why It Matters, and How to Harness It, Crown, Random House, New York, N.Y., 2021

Kubler-Ross, Elizabeth and Kessler, David, *Life Lessons,* Scribner, New York, 2000.

Laney, Marti Olsen, *The Introvert Advantage, How to Thrive in an Extrovert World,* Workman Publishing, New York.

Leal, Bento C., *4 Essential Keys to Effective Communication,* Bento C. Leal lll, 2017.

Lerner, Harriet, PhD. *The Dance of Connection, How to Talk to Someone When You're Mad, Hurt, Scared, Frustrated, Insulted, Betrayed, or Desperate.,* HarperCollins, 2001.

Matsumoto, David, Frank Mark, and Hwang, Hyi Sung, *Nonverbal Communication, Science and Applications,* Sage, Thousand Oaks, Ca., 2013.

Matousek, Mark, *Sex, Death, and Enlightenment, Riverhead Books, New York, N.Y., 1996*

Maxwell, John C., *The 5 Levels of Leadership*, Hachette Book Group, New York, N.Y., 2021.

Millman, Dan, *Way of the Peaceful Warrior,* New World Library, Novato, Ca. 2000

Mipham, Sakyom, *The Lost Art of Good Conversation,* Harmony Books, Penguin Random House, 2017.

Nepo, Mark, *The Book of Awakening,* Red Wheel/Weiser LLC, Newburyport, MA., 2020

Nisrgadatta Maharaj, *I am That*, The Acorn Press, Durham, NC; 2nd American edition (revised) edition (August 8, 2012).

Obama, Barack, *A Promised Land*, Crown Publishing, 2020.

Pease, Allan and Barbara, *The Definitive Book of Body Language*, Bantam Books, 2006

Reynolds, Marcia, *Outsmart Your Brain*, Covisioning, Phoenix, AZ., 2017.

Rubin, Gretchen, *The Four Tendencies: The Indispensable Personality Profiles That Reveal How to Make Your Life Better (and Other People's Lives Better, Too)*, Harmony Books, Penguin Random House, 2017.

Schwerdtfeger, *Keynote Mastery, The Personal Journal of a Professional Speaker*, Authority Publishing, Gold River, Ca., 2016.

Senge, Peter, *The Fifth Discipline, Currency Books*, N.Y.,N.Y. 2006

Sesno, Frank, *Ask More: The Power of Questions to Open Doors, Uncover Solutions, and Spark Change*, American Management Association, New York, 2017.

Stone, Douglas et al., *Difficult Conversations*, Penguin Books, New York, N.Y., 2000.

Tuhovsky, Ian, *The Science of Effective Communication*, 2017.

Tull, Anna Huckabee, *Living the Deeper YES: Discovering the finest, Truest Place within You*, Balboa Press, Bloomington, IN. 47403.

Turkle, Sherry, *Reclaiming Conversation, The Power of Talk in a Digital Age*, Penguin Books, New York, N.Y., 2016.

Wise, Will et al. *Ask Powerful Questions*, 2017, Round Table Companies, Deerfield, Il.

Endnotes

[1] Research results taken from publicly available survey, Conversational Style Guide, ©petergibb, further details in Chapter 3

[2] https://www.bbc.com/news/world, June 24, 2018. More every day.

[3] Yo Yo Ma

[4] Mindfulness meditation: A research-proven way to reduce stress, https://www.apa.org/topics/mindfulness/meditation, Oct 30, 2019

[5] This term has been used by others with various meanings, and appears now in discussions of on line dialogues, see Faridah Pawan, Indiana University et al, "Interventions and Student Factors in Collaboration,"

[6] The term "Personal Meaning" is used in psychotherapy, particularly in what is sometimes referred to as "meaning therapy." See https://www.meaning.ca/meaning-centred-interventions/meaning-therapy/

[7] For another view of this 3 tiered model, see Stone, Douglas et al., *Difficult Conversations,* Penguin Books, New York, N.Y.,2000

[8] If you want to further explore the subject of conversation starters, you can have a ball with this one on the Internet. search away. Have fun.

[9] The distinction between speaking and listening is often confused with introversion and extroversion. There is certain a relationship,

but the two sets of concepts are not synonymous. For the best exploration of introversion and extroversion, I recommend Suisan Cain's wonderful book, Quiet, Broadway Books, New York, 2012.

[10] The Neuroscience of Everybody's Favorite Topic, Alan Ward, Scientific American, July 16, 2013

[11] I draw on the work of Martin Buber, Israeli philosopher, here. See *I and Thou,* Simon & Schuster, 1970, N.Y., N.Y.

[12] The research and evidence for the positive impact of effective listening is sold. See, for example, "What Great Listeners Actually Do," Jack Zenger and Joseph Folkman, Harvard Business Review, July 2016.

[13] Many have attempted to pinpoint the exact % relationship of impact of nonverbal vs verbal communication. I think its a fool's errand.

[14] Lots of scholarly articles address the issue, see for example, Regina Pally M.D., A Primary Role for Nonverbal Communication in Psychoanalysis, in Psychoanalytic Inquiry, July 2008

[15] This chapter is a survey of the various tools of non-verbal communication. It is not exhaustive. If you want to delve deeper into this subject, there are a number of fine books that go beyond what I can cover here. A favorite is *The Definitive Book of Body Language: The Hidden Meaning Behind People's Gestures and Expressions,* Allan and Barbara Pease, Bantam Books, 2004

[16] Helen Reiss, The Science of Empathy, Journal of Patient Experience. June 2017

[17] Whether it was really Thomas Gordon's Parent Effectiveness Training model or Carl Roger's, Client Centered Therapy that most pioneered the "I Statement" language appears to be in some doubt. But does it matter. Both men contributed enormously to our understanding of effective, non-coercive communications.

[18] The Experiment in International Living

[19] (https://rightquestion.org/)

[20] Will Wise, Chad Littlefield, *Ask Powerful Questions: Create Conversations That Matter,* Round Table Companies, Deerfield, Il., 2017

[21] Nicklas Balboa, Three Habits That Reduce Conversational Success, Psychology Today, September 2020

[22] Kross, Ethan, *Chatter, The Voice in our Head, Why It Matters, and How to Harness It,* 2021, Crown, New York, N.Y.

[23] Barrett, Lisa Feldman PhD., How Emotions Are Made: The Secret Life of the Brain, Mariner Books, HarperCollins.

[24] Not all neuroscientists agree on the powers of the amygdala. See Lisa Feldman Barrett, *Seven and a Half Lessons About the Brain,* Mariner Books, 2021.

[25] Ensler, Eve, The Apology, 2019, Bloomsbury Books.

[26] Brach, Tara, *Radical Acceptance: Embracing Your Life With the Heart of a Buddha,* 2004, Bantam Dell, New York, N.Y.

[27] *I draw here again from Ethan Kross, Chatter: The Voice in our Head, Why It Matters, and How to Harness It.*

[28] Mark Nepo, Book of Awakening, 2020, Red Wheel/Weiser LLC, Newburyport, MA.

Acknowledgments

This book lives on the shoulders of so many writers, thinkers and inspiring leaders who have come before me. Too numerous to list here, but I have tried to give credit to a number throughout the book.

I would like to thank the two stalwart members of my critique group who read through early drafts and gave such valuable feedback: David Widup and John French. You were editors, colleagues and friends to me in the era of the blank page. I can still hear your always encouraging and always straight feedback in my ear. Many thanks for all.

A good editor is a writer's best friend, and I have had the benefit of several, starting with Elisa Page. The support I received from Atmosphere Press was enormously valuable, special thanks go to Alex Kale and Trista Page, without whom this book would still be a shadow of the final product. I also benefitted greatly from the support from Cam Finch, Ronaldo Alves, Evan Courtright, and Erin Larson-Burnett, all delightful professionals who played key roles in converting a somewhat raggedy manuscript into a real book.

About Atmosphere Press

Atmosphere Press is an independent, full-service publisher for excellent books in all genres and for all audiences. Learn more about what we do at atmospherepress.com.

We encourage you to check out some of Atmosphere's latest releases, which are available at Amazon.com and via order from your local bookstore:

Portal or Hole: Meditations on Art, Religion, Race and the Pandemic, by Pamela M. Connell

A Walk Through the Wilderness, by Dan Conger

The House at 104: Memoir of a Childhood, by Anne Hegnauer

A Short History of Newton Hall, Chester, by Chris Fozzard

Serial Love: When Happily Ever After... Isn't, by Kathy Kay

Sit-Ins, Drive-Ins, and Uncle Sam, by Bill Slawter

Black Water and Tulips, by Sara Mansfield Taber

Ghosted: Dating & Other Paramoural Experiences, by Jana Eisenstein

FLAWED HOUSES of FOUR SEASONS, by James Morris

About the Author

I grew up without Mindful Conversation. I know the cost.

I was a shy kid who morphed into an awkward teen and then hung out for a decade or so in the adult lost and found. I thought of myself as a relationship failure, an introvert trying to become an extrovert. Once I'd learned what a foolish mission that was, life changed. I discovered a new me, one who actually had a lot to say.

And people now wanted to talk to me. I boarded a train bound for Curiosity, Creativity and Freedom. That train has taken me through countryside more beautiful than I ever could have imagined.

I'm still an introvert at heart. I spend a lot of time happily alone — thinking, reading, writing, composing songs, playing my guitar, dreaming, meditating, hiking, getting ever more clear about which questions I want to ask, even if I never find answers. It's about the journey. I'm a creativity junkie. I thrive on those moments when I feel a deep connection with another, or when I feel the magic of discovery in my veins, when I am being most fully me, expressing myself openly, authentically, lovingly.

I live in Ashland, OR, with my dear wife, Wendy. We have three children and five grandchildren, all thankfully living within a day's drive from our home. Post Covid, I will get a chance to exercise my arms again, with hugs abundant all around. Lots of pets in the past. Right now, none, but we had two fawns born in our yard this year. New growth is everywhere.